Bartolomé de las Casas and the Conquest of the Americas

Viewpoints/Puntos de Vista
Themes and Interpretations in Latin American History

Series editor: Jürgen Buchenau

The books in this series will introduce students to the most significant themes and topics in Latin American history. They represent a novel approach to designing supplementary texts for this growing market. Intended as supplementary textbooks, the books will also discuss the ways in which historians have interpreted these themes and topics, thus demonstrating to students that our understanding of our past is constantly changing, through the emergence of new sources, methodologies, and historical theories. Unlike monographs, the books in this series will be broad in scope and written in a style accessible to undergraduates.

Published

A History of the Cuban Revolution
Aviva Chomsky

Bartolomé de las Casas and the Conquest of the Americas
Lawrence A. Clayton

Mexican Immigration to the United States
Timothy J. Henderson

In preparation

The Last Caudillo: Alvaro Obregón and the Mexican Revolution
Jürgen Buchenau

Creoles vs. Peninsulars in Colonial Spanish America
Mark Burkholder

Dictatorship in South America
Jerry Davila

Mexico Since 1940: The Unscripted Revolution
Stephen E. Lewis

The Haitian Revolution, 1791–1804
Jeremy Popkin

Bartolomé de las Casas and the Conquest of the Americas

Lawrence A. Clayton

WILEY-BLACKWELL

A John Wiley & Sons, Ltd., Publication

Blackwell Publishing was acquired by John Wiley & Sons in February 2007. Blackwell's publishing program has been merged with Wiley's global Scientific, Technical, and Medical business to form Wiley-Blackwell.

Registered Office
John Wiley & Sons Ltd, The Atrium, Southern Gate, Chichester, West Sussex, PO19 8SQ, United Kingdom

Editorial Offices
350 Main Street, Malden, MA 02148-5020, USA
9600 Garsington Road, Oxford, OX4 2DQ, UK
The Atrium, Southern Gate, Chichester, West Sussex, PO19 8SQ, UK

For details of our global editorial offices, for customer services, and for information about how to apply for permission to reuse the copyright material in this book please see our website at www.wiley.com/wiley-blackwell.

Library of Congress Cataloging-in-Publication Data

Clayton, Lawrence A.
  Bartolomé de las Casas and the conquest of the Americas / Lawrence A. Clayton.
      p. cm.—(Viewpoints/puntos de vista : themes and interpretations in Latin American history)
  Includes bibliographical references and index.
  ISBN 978-1-4051-9427-3 (hardcover : alk. paper)—
ISBN 978-1-4051-9428-0 (pbk. : alk. paper)   1. Casas, Bartolomé de las, 1474–1566.   2. America–Discovery and exploration–Spanish.   3. Indians, Treatment of–Latin America–History.   4. Slavery–America–History–16th century.   5. Slave trade–America–History–16th century.   6. Casas, Bartolomé de las, 1474–1566.   I. Title.
  E125.C4C53 2011
  972'.02092–dc22
  [B]

                                                                    2010030304

A catalogue record for this book is available from the British Library.

Set in 10/12.5 pt Minion by Toppan Best-set Premedia Limited

1   2011

This volume is dedicated to the memory of Bartolomé de las Casas and the Taino peoples of the Caribbean, whose suffering led to his life's calling as protector of American Indians.

Contents

List of Illustrations

Maps

Figures

Series Editor's Preface

Each book in the "Viewpoints/Puntos de Vista" series introduces students to a significant theme or topic in Latin American history. In an age in which student and faculty interest in the developing world increasingly challenges the old focus on the history of Europe and North America, Latin American history has assumed an increasingly prominent position in undergraduate curricula.

Some of these books discuss the ways in which historians have interpreted these themes and topics, thus demonstrating that our understanding of our past is constantly changing, through the emergence of new sources, methodologies, and historical theories. Others offer an introduction to a particular theme by means of a case study or biography in a manner easily understood by the contemporary, non-specialist reader. Yet others give an overview of a major theme that might serve as the foundation of an upper-level course.

What is common to all of these books is their goal of historical synthesis by drawing on the insights of generations of scholarship on the most enduring and fascinating issues in Latin American history, and through the use of primary sources as appropriate. Each book is written by a specialist in Latin American history who is concerned with undergraduate teaching, yet who has also made his or her mark as a first-rate scholar.

The books in this series can be used in a variety of ways, recognizing the differences in teaching conditions at small liberal arts colleges, large public universities, and research-oriented institutions with doctoral programs. Faculty have particular needs depending on whether they teach large lectures with discussion sections, small lecture or discussion-oriented classes, or large lectures with no discussion sections, and whether they teach on a semester or trimester system. The format adopted for this series fits all of these different parameters.

This volume is one of the two inaugural books in the "Viewpoints/Puntos de Vista" series. In *Bartolomé de las Casas and the Conquest of the Americas*, Larry Clayton recounts the life and times of a Spaniard who arrived in the New World with his father in the early days of colonization and conquest. After he witnessed firsthand the cruelty of colonialism as the owner of an *encomienda*, Las Casas abandoned his worldly career for a calling as a Dominican friar. He became the most vociferous critic of Spanish abuses in the New World, and particularly the practice of enslavement of the indigenous population. Based on Las Casas's own writings and a close reading of the historical literature, Clayton provides a sympathetic yet trenchant biography that serves as an entry into the larger issues of colonialism, slavery, indigenous resistance, and the early colonial debate about human rights in Latin America.

Jurgen Buchenau
University of North Carolina, Charlotte

Acknowledgments

While researching and writing this work, I have been helped by many friends and colleagues and institutions, none of whom are in any way responsible for errors in fact or judgment that may have survived in this small book in spite of their good efforts. Institutionally, the University of Alabama provided me with two sabbaticals, one in 1998 and one in 2005, without which I could not have initiated or completed this study. The Pew Evangelical Scholars Program (now discontinued) supported me in a full year of research in 1999–2000 that was indispensable.

Individually, many of my colleagues and students at the University of Alabama were supportive and helpful, reading portions of the manuscript, answering questions on recondite corners of history, always encouraging me. Among those are Tony Clark (now at Whitworth University), Maarten Ultee (emeritus), Jimmy Mixson, Dave Michelson, Steve Bunker, George McClure, Michael Mendle, James Knight, Steve Newton, and especially Helen Delpar for reading and commenting on the entire manuscript.

Others across the Atlantic world whom I have leaned on for comments, advice, and support are John L. Schwaller, Salvador Larrúa Guedes, G. Douglas Inglis, Lynne Guitar, Jesús Rodríguez, S.J., Stafford Poole, C.M., Eyda M. Merediz, Daniel Castro, and Santa Arias.

At Wiley-Blackwell, my editor and his assistant, Peter Coveney and Galen Smith, were immensely supportive and I thank them for their enthusiasm, both professional and personal. Thanks to Jane Taylor, picture researcher in the UK, who helped us track down such esoterica as permissions from dead art collectors and reclusive friars.

Jürgen Buchenau, the general editor of the series, at the University of North Carolina-Charlotte, and I first exchanged some ideas on this book at a meeting of the South Eastern Council on Latin American Studies (SECOLAS) in Ybor City, Tampa, one beautiful spring day in 2008.

Jürgen encouraged me to join him as he planned this series Viewpoints. We agreed that there was no more seminal—or controversial—figure than Bartolomé de Las Casas in early Latin American history and he was the perfect vehicle for opening this series on differing perspectives and points of view in the making of Latin America.

And at home, close to my heart and my office, my wife Louise and son Carlton have patiently put up with dad once again obsessed by some historical figure or subject, this time the friar Las Casas for over ten years that I will admit to.

Timeline

1537	Pope Paul III's Bull on American Indians
1540	Return to Spain, Las Casas
1542	Publication of New Laws for governing the Indies
1543	Las Casas appointed Bishop of Chiapa
1544	Las Casas's fourth trip to the Indies
1544–47	In Guatemala, New Spain
1545–63	Council of Trent meets
1547	Las Casas returns to Spain
1550–51	Debate between Las Casas and Ginés de Sepúlveda
1552	Las Casas publishes major tracts, Seville
1553–61	Las Casas in Valladolid
1561–66	Las Casas in Madrid
1566	Death of Las Casas[1]

---

[1] All dates relating to Las Casas largely from Isacio Pérez Fernández, O. P. *Cronologia documentada de los viajes, estancias y actuaciones de Fray Bartolomé de las Casas* (Bayamon, Puerto Rico: Centro de Estudios de los Dominicos del Caribe, Universidad Central de Bayamon, 1984), supplemented by Helen Rand Parish, *Las Casas en México* (Mexico, 1992).

Introduction

The age of the exploration and conquest of the Americas has undergone some remarkable changes in interpretation in the past half century. This short book will serve as an introduction to this seminal period in world history encompassed by the fifteenth and sixteenth centuries.

You will read about traditional and modern interpretations of what happened, and how historians and other students of the past such as archaeologists, ethnographers, and demographers have defined and studied the changes in world history prompted by this great encounter between two worlds. As the distinguished historian John Parry once observed, "America was not discovered by the Europeans; it was truly a meeting of two cultures who had not known each other previously."[1]

Most readers are familiar with some of the bare facts of the age of the conquest: the discoveries made by Christopher Columbus; the beginning of the European settlements on the large islands of the Caribbean, and then the continuing conquest of lands and Amerindian peoples across the continents of North America and South America and including the connecting isthmus of Central America.[2] But as researchers have probed more deeply into the documentation and have embraced new priorities and brought new perspectives into the equation of interpreting the past, it seems that the history of the Conquest has been loosened from its foundations and radiates with controversy and differing points of view.

Bartolomé de las Casas and the Conquest of the Americas. Lawrence A. Clayton
© 2011 Lawrence A. Clayton

For example, to label it the "Conquest" of America is hardly acceptable to a new generation of scholars. It was, as John Parry noted, a meeting of two worlds, an encounter between two civilizations, and you will often find "Encounter" used as a substitute for "Conquest." In this book, we will use both, for each has a special meaning. *Conquest* implies a superiority of one civilization over the other, while *encounter* implies a greater equality of customs and culture, each different in many ways but neither "superior" in overall qualities. That the Spanish and Portuguese wielded a technological and military superiority over most of the Amerindian peoples, from the village-level people of the Caribbean to the great state-level Archaic empires of the Aztec in Mexico and Inca in Peru, is generally true, and thus "conquest" by arms is appropriate.[3] But even within this category, there is disagreement. The Spanish, armed with swords of Toledan steel and great war horses, did not simply ride roughshod over Amerindians armed with primitive weapons, absolutely intimidating and overwhelming the Tainos, for example, on the island of Española or the Aztecs of central Mexico. The first "battle" or campaign between the Tainos and Spaniards on Española went to the Tainos, and the mighty conquistador of the Aztecs, Hernán Cortés, waged a campaign of fire and terror between 1519 and 1523 on the Aztecs, the outcome of which was not a given. The Aztec warriors gave as much as they took and the pendulum of battle swung back and forth, driven by courage, wile, terror, technology, and disease, all in different proportions at different times of the campaign.

The first chronicles or histories of any given era—such as the Encounter—are usually the ones to establish the "orthodox" or traditional view of what happened. History is based on documentary evidence, which by definition is based on written records. Since the Spanish were literate and the great bulk of the Indian population was not, the first chronicles and records of the Conquest were produced by Spaniards. Their point of view was celebratory and triumphant, while the Indian perspective was submerged or highly skewed, seen through the lens of Spanish customs and traditions.

The Spanish, or Eurocentric, perspective is challenged by contradictory evidence and points of view, many of them recent, born of new scholarship, but some perspectives—as you will read shortly below—arise from eyewitness accounts by Spaniards of the epoch itself. Some of these eyewitnesses did not view the Conquest as the unvarnished triumph of Spanish culture and Christianity over Amerindian barbarism and paganism. Other issues dot the landscape of the Encounter.

We do not really know how many people inhabited the Americas when Columbus completed his first voyage: Twenty-five million? Fifty million? One hundred million? More? Nor are we sure how devastating the role of diseases—largely European ones to which Amerindians had no immunities—played in the eventual predominance of the Spanish military conquest of the Americas. Scholars in the mid-twentieth century, led by a group of demographers, ethnographers, geographers, and historians at the University of California, determined with some precision—they thought—that the scythe of European epidemic diseases, such as smallpox, laid waste the Amerindian populations and thus made possible the swift conquest of the Americas. It certainly helped to have "General Smallpox" marching alongside Hernán Cortés into Mexico, or with Francisco Pizarro into Peru in 1532, but recent scholarship has considerably downplayed the role of disease and instead substituted the growing weight of European settlers to the Americas as a factor in the Encounter.[4] Even the widespread assertion that a smallpox pandemic spread with terrifying rapidity across Mexico and Peru has been questioned in the light of studies on the actual spread of the disease—usually slowly and only among families, household members and others who had to be in close contact with an infected person. Reports of the spread and devastating effects of smallpox, as described by chroniclers, and accepted by historians of the twentieth century looking to the germs and diseases theory to account for the rapidity of the Spanish Conquest, simply do not conform to how smallpox spreads.[5]

The legends of the Spanish conquistadors have been persistent, given life by the accounts of the Spanish themselves of course.[6] Did the Amerindians really consider the European strangers to be gods in some human form? Were Amerindians religions so different from the Roman Catholicism that came in with the Spaniards? Did these same Spaniards truly think of the Amerindians as a lesser form of humankind?

These and other questions, and how they are addressed and answered, come broadly under the category of historiography, which is the study of how historians over the ages have interpreted the facts. In the pages that follow, you will find three basic elements, all essential to any good history: first, a presentation of the basics of the exploration, discovery, and conquest of the Americas; second, a presentation and discussion of the differing interpretations of what it all actually means—often very nuanced but sometimes radically different; and third, woven into all of this, the life of one man, Bartolomé de las Casas (1485–1566), to give this history a human face. Las Casas, however, was no ordinary Spanish settler in the "Indies" (a term employed by the Spanish to describe the Americas, along with the "New World" occasionally).[7]

Arguably the most important person of the age after Christopher Columbus (1451–1506), Las Casas was involved at almost every stage, major event, or controversy of the Conquest in one fashion or another. Las Casas, who became a priest and later a Dominican friar, was formed by the powerful forces of the epoch. But he was also a principal actor and eyewitness to the Conquest, and his writings and hot rhetoric helped fashion how Europeans and Amerindians clashed and adapted to each other in the unique environment following Columbus's first voyage 1492–1493. As one of his contemporaries noted, "He is a candle that lights everything in sight!"[8] And unlike Columbus, who only became celebrated centuries after his death, Las Casas achieved notoriety among his fellow countrymen in his lifetime because of his radical stands in defense of the Indians.

At the core of his life was an almost fanatical defense of the Indians in the face of the Spanish Conquest, sometimes labeled an "invasion" by modern students, and certainly seen so by the Indians. The settler/conquistador class lambasted Las Casas as a traitor to his race for pandering to the pagan Indians, whose religious culture included human sacrifice and ritual cannibalism, considered obscenities by Christians.

Las Casas defended the Indians with equal hyperbole, exaggerating their virtues and denouncing Spanish atrocities and the seemingly wanton destruction of an innocent people. When one reads accounts or descriptions of Las Casas's actions or life, either written by critics or defenders in his own lifetime or produced five hundred years later in the twenty-first century, it is often like reading about two different people. In his lifetime, he divided people with his radical philosophical and theological interpretations and actions; in modern times he has been both edified and vilified. Some consider him a traitor to the Spanish nation;

others are sponsoring a move to beatify him in preparation to name him a saint in the Catholic Church.

Las Casas first traveled to the Indies, to Santo Domingo, the capital of the growing Spanish colony of Española (today the island shared by the Dominican Republic and Haiti) in 1502 with his father, who was returning to the Indies for the second time as a merchant. Then, only about 18, he had already decided to enter the clergy and had started down the road to priesthood by taking minor orders. In that sense, he represented one of the great streams contributing to the forthcoming conquest of the Americas, the spiritual one. The Church, Roman Catholicism being the religion of Spain, played an immense role in the nature and process of the Spanish Conquest of the Indies, or, putting the event into a larger context, the European encounter with and reaction to a new world where the people did not know Christianity and worshipped in many different ways. Las Casas and his clerical peers who went to the Indies in this early period fervently sought to evangelize and convert the Indians to Christianity, and the story of Las Casas's efforts is representative of the whole phenomenon of the evangelization of the Indians over the next half century, especially by members of the three great religious orders of the times, the Franciscans, Dominicans, and Augustinians.

If Christianity represented one stream contributing to the river of Spaniards traveling to the Americas, another one was the role of his father as a merchant and trader. Like Columbus, the son of a Genoese merchant who traded throughout the Mediterranean world, Las Casas and his father were part of a merchant family whose fortunes rose and fell on the ships and goods they traded throughout the world as it was known to them at the end of the fifteenth century. The Spaniards and Portuguese made a good living at buying, transporting, and selling goods, from African slaves to sugar, across the nexus of Atlantic ports and merchants. The horizons of these merchants were expanded considerably by Portuguese explorations and trade down the coast of Africa in the fifteenth century and by Columbus's truly revolutionary voyage across the Atlantic near the end of that century. Las Casas and his contemporaries were there, in fact, at the opening of a historical phenomenon now known more precisely as the "Atlantic World." As Thomas Benjamin noted, "Prior to the fifteenth century, the peoples, societies, and politics in the Americas, Africa, and Europe had little or no contact with one another."[9] Columbus's voyage, and the continuing exploration for trade and commerce down the African coast and out into the Atlantic islands by the Portuguese, changed that world from one of relative provinciality and isolation to one of connections, change, and growth. "The arrival of Europeans in West Africa and in the Americas," Benjamin wrote, "transformed the lives and destinies of Africans and Indians, sometimes for better and more often for worse ... the Atlantic World became a New World for all."

Las Casas and his contemporaries were heirs as well of another tradition deeply imbedded into the psyche of Christian Spain. As a boy, he had grown up in the age of the great Catholic sovereigns of Spain— Queen Isabel of Castile and her husband King Ferdinand of Aragon—on the verge of seizing the last Moorish kingdom of Granada in Iberia in 1492, and thus completing the long Reconquest of Spain for Christendom. Muslim peoples from Africa had crossed over the Straits of Gibraltar almost eight hundred years earlier, in 711 AD, and conquered most of the Iberian peninsula for Islam. Beginning around the year 1000, small Christian kingdoms in the far north of Iberia, along the coast facing the Bay of Biscay and the Atlantic Ocean, began a series of raids and invasions that kicked off the long almost five hundred year era of the Reconquest of Spain for Christendom. The Reconquest imbued Spain with a curious attitude of tolerance among Christians, Jews, and Moors (the term used by the Spanish to refer to Muslims and their descendants in Spain) in the medieval period, but that tolerance gradually gave way to a militant, intolerant Christianity by 1492.

The long period of intermittent but often brutal warfare between Christians and Moors over the centuries produced a hard, almost contemptuous disregard for life and the suffering of individuals caught in the cauldron of war. When the Spaniards of the Reconquest reached the Indies, they carried with them their habits of war, and they forced the Tainos of the island of Española to submit to their authority in the same fashion in which they had brought the Moors of Granada to their knees. Las Casas witnessed the "reduction" (a euphemism favored by the conquistadors) of the island's inhabitants to obedience to work in the mines extracting gold, thinly disguised by the rationalization that this was necessary to bring Christianity to the Indians. Las Casas recorded a great deal of what he witnessed and this documentary evidence became the source of the "Black Legend," the fiction or fact (depending upon your point of view) that the Spanish were uniquely cruel and insensitive in their encounter with the Amerindians across the Americas.

The counterargument to the Black Legend was the White Legend. It came into existence in the twentieth century, constructed by patriotic Spaniards to counter the Hispanophobic Black Legend that had been used by Protestants in Spain's rival European states, especially England, to batter the image of Catholic Spain in the many wars of competition among European nations over the centuries. The White Legend argued that Spain was no worse than her English, French, and Dutch rivals in their invasions of America, and that, in fact, the bringing of Christianity— with a few excesses acknowledged, given the innate corruption of man—to the Amerindians freed them from the deceptions of the devil and endowed them with eternal salvation.[10] If there were ever two almost diametrically opposed points of view, they can be seen in how people over the ages—of all nationalities and across the five centuries—have interpreted the nature of the conquest of the Americas. And providing much of the documentary evidence, through his writings, was Las Casas.

There has been, for example, a recent trend in scholarship attributing a great deal of "agency" to Amerindians in the course of the conquest and settlement of the Americas. This means simply that the Amerindians were able to, and did, act on their own behalf a lot more than has heretofore been ascribed to them by standard accounts of the Conquest. For example, they preserved many of their religious practices and customs even in the face of the demands of the Spanish to convert and conform to Christianity. "Agency" has been attributed in many other realms— language, food, gender, legal traditions, political structures, and family values—to the continuing existence of an Amerindian culture in many parts of the Americas, so much so that someone reading of Amerindian agency might be tempted to think that the Conquest was not so bad after all.[11] Of course, one has to investigate specific areas at specific times, for overarching generalizations will obscure competing points of view.

The experiences of the Taino Indians on the island of Española are very different from those of the Incas in the southern highlands of Peru, for example. The latter survived, while the former did not. There are no direct descendants of the Taino in the modern Dominican Republic or

Haiti. On the other hand, Inca descendants number in the millions in southern Peru and in neighboring Bolivia, and all along the highlands of the Andes into Ecuador. Were the dynamics of the Conquest so different in the Greater Antilles (the large islands in the Caribbean of Cuba, Española, Puerto Rico, and Jamaica) than in the high valleys of the Andes, or in the heart of Mexico, where hundreds of thousands, perhaps millions, survived the Conquest?

In fact, few Amerindians—whether the village-level Tainos of Española or the state-level Incas of the great capital city of Cuzco—viewed the coming of the Spanish as anything more than some unmitigated evil inflicted on them by circumstances or gods.[12] As Las Casas recorded, they died on the islands by the hundreds, then the thousands, and then the tens of thousands as the exploration, discovery, and conquest proceeded through the Greater Antilles, eventually reaching the mainlands of Mexico, Central America, North America, and South America within twenty years of Columbus's first voyage. Las Casas's critics claim he exaggerated the toll, the pain, the injury, the injustice, and the cruelty of the conquistadors, and, in doing so, indicted his own race, while grossly extolling the virtues of the Amerindians. What, in fact, was Las Casas's point of view?

Las Casas was acting well within a powerful tradition in Christianity, the role of prophet. He has been described as historian, biographer, proto-anthropologist, chronicler, social activist, advocate, and, of course, writer. He was all of those, but, overriding all of those, he was a prophet in the model of the Old Testament, sent by God "to go out and preach to his people, usually for the purpose of calling them back from some errant way."[13] Prophets saw themselves not as seers or forecasters of the future, but as messengers picked out by God.

Was Las Casas called by God, in some vision or mystical experience similar to the prophets of the Old Testament? Las Casas certainly thought so, as you will read below in the experience he credits with his call as prophet.[14] And, as Stafford Poole noted, once called, "the call cannot be rejected."[15] Like Jeremiah and others, Las Casas was compelled to carry out his mission, in his case, protecting the Indians of the Americas.

Another characteristic of the prophet was to see things in black and white, in absolutes. Compromises may be required in pursuit of the goal, but were not acceptable in the long run. Prophets, to further their mission, often described themselves, their enemies and the world around them in extremes, using superlatives and hyperbole, exaggerating virtues and vices. To further his vision, the prophet, and this was especially true of Las Casas, recorded the events he had witnessed, or read about, in his lifetime and in doing so also became one of the principal chronicler/ historians of the Conquest.[16]

What Las Casas witnessed on the island of Española between 1502– 1511 (and wrote about in his *History of the Indies*) determined the course of his life: defending the Amerindians from the abuses inflicted upon them by the Spanish. He returned to Spain on at least four occasions in his lifetime, each time to seek the support of the Crown and like-thinking allies, especially among the Dominicans and Franciscans, and he became the most outspoken, well-known protector of Amerindians before the forums of power in Spain.

In doing all this—as friar, prophet, and protector of Indians—Las Casas's life provides a core experience, from his arrival in the New World in 1502, to his death in 1566, to explore the foundations of Spain's empire in the Americas. His life spanned almost exactly the age of exploration, discovery, and conquest. But, while his life gives us the thread and gateway into the history of the Conquest, it was not Las Casas, but Christopher Columbus who kicked it off.

1

The Era of Columbus and the "Discoverers"

Christopher Columbus arrived in Las Casas's hometown of Seville on Palm Sunday, March 31, 1493. The Admiral was on a triumphal passage through Spain on his way to meet the sovereigns, Isabel and Ferdinand, in Barcelona after returning from his historic first voyage. Columbus was expected for High Mass at the cathedral, and Sevillans gathered in the center of the city to get a good view of the Admiral and his entourage.

With Columbus marched eight to ten Taino Indians captured in the Caribbean. Dressed in their native feathers and fishbone and gold ornaments, they drew curious stares from the onlookers, as much impressed by the accompanying parrots as the strange "Indians." Young Bartolomé de las Casas, then eight years old, witnessed the procession into the city. The procession could hardly have been missed. Even in Spain, where the horse was the fastest form of transportation, the news of the Admiral's return from his voyage spread rapidly through the many kingdoms of medieval Spain—Castile, León, Aragón, Valencia—united by the marriage of King Ferdinand of Aragón and Queen Isabel of Castile in 1469. Early modern Spain was emerging as these two forged the links of a powerful monarchy, but a Spaniard of the age of the Crusades hundreds of years earlier would have recognized his land and its people easily. Change came about slowly in the medieval world, but the first voyage of

Bartolomé de las Casas and the Conquest of the Americas. Lawrence A. Clayton
© 2011 Lawrence A. Clayton

Columbus detonated an explosion of knowledge that transformed that world.

Columbus had sailed west and discovered some islands on the other side of the Atlantic Ocean. Las Casas's father, Pedro de las Casas, a small merchant with large ambitions, joined Columbus on his second voyage in 1493, while two uncles, Francisco de Peñalosa and Juan, soon also became involved with the Admiral, as Columbus was now being called. The Genoese explorer's star rose rapidly through the ranks of Spanish sailors and merchants ever since the King and Queen had summoned him to Barcelona and granted him the privileges and rank he desired.

Columbus continued from Seville on his triumphant trip to Barcelona, mobbed by curious sightseers and well-wishers, to say nothing of potential gentlemen adventurers seeking favor and a place on the next voyage. The news of the Admiral's voyage rapidly spread across the plains and mountains of the many kingdoms of Spain. Only one year previously the Queen and King had finally defeated the last Moors (Muslims from Africa) of Spain in Granada and completed the centuries-long Reconquest of Spain for Christendom. The men of Castile dreamed of being knights in the Queen's Castilian army, charging into battle with the standards of the great Spanish warrior saint, Santiago, unfurled in the wind, to slay infidels in the name of the true Holy Catholic faith. That they also were most interested in gaining wealth and honor in a decidedly secular fashion, even while making their way up in the spiritual hierarchy of Christendom by slaying Moors, was just as true. The Reconquest was a way of life in which one gained prizes, wealth, slaves, land, titles, and honor through war.

This long Reconquest rises above all other affairs at the end of the fifteenth century. As mentioned in the Introduction, in AD 711, a wave of Muslims crossed the eight-and-a-half-mile strait dividing Africa from Europe. Commanded by Tariq ibn Ziyad, these 12,000 invaders soon conquered almost all of Iberia. Gibraltar (Jabal al Tariq, or the mount of Tarik) still bears the imprint of this long-ago invasion. For a few hundred years, an uneasy but prosperous peace ensued in Iberia among Christians, Muslims, and Jews.[1] Indeed, a bright center of civilization sparkled around the caliphate and city of Córdoba in southern Spain. Córdoba became the richest and most powerful state in all Europe. Around the year 1000 AD, the Reconquest of the peninsula began in earnest, led by small Christian kingdoms in the north that had survived the Muslim invasion.

The Reconquest stamped Spain with a martial culture. After nearly five hundred years of intermittent warfare, the only surviving Moorish kingdom was Granada on the southeastern corner of the Iberian peninsula, and Granada fell in January, 1492. The triumph of Ferdinand and Isabel was a triumph of the militant Church, and the two—Christianity and arms—were indelibly linked in the Spanish consciousness of the age.

But Columbus, who emerges preeminent in the history of the period, was no warrior.[2] He represented a different, powerful tradition in Europe emerging in the fifteenth century, led by Portuguese explorers and merchants. Driven by commercial desire to expand the boundaries of trade beyond the Iberian peninsula, and with increasingly effective technological developments in the tools of navigation and sailing, the Portuguese pushed down the African coast for most of the fifteenth century until they rounded Cape of Good Hope in 1488, opening the way for sailing into the Indian Ocean and beyond by the end of the century.[3] Columbus sailed for a number of years in the service of Portugal into the ports and harbors of the Atlantic—all the way from Iceland to Africa—during this period of expansion. This move from the relative provincialism and insularity of the European medieval period into a dynamic epoch of exploration, discovery, and trade has usually been labeled the era of "early modern Europe." The stage for the emergence of early modern Portugal or Spain was the Atlantic world, another modern paradigm which emphasizes the growing connectivity among islands and continents bordering the great Atlantic Ocean. And Columbus was the quintessential navigator, merchant, explorer, and discoverer of this age.

In his life we see converging all of these different elements that contributed to the making of early modern Spain. Among these were the mercantile tradition, the technological advantages in sailing and navigation, the powerful religious dimension, and, perhaps underscoring them all, the entrepreneurial spirit of change that drove these communities of navigators, merchant princes, bankers, and kings and queens to push beyond the old geographical and cultural boundaries of Europe into the Atlantic world.

The religious fervor of the Reconquest, seen as carrying over into and deeply influencing the later conquest of the Americas, has long received the most attention by historians. In a spate of religious zealotry, Jews were expelled (unless they chose to convert) from Spain in 1492, and ten years later all Moors were forced to convert to Christianity or choose exile, the same as the Jews. Ethnically and racially this was an intolerant society. The Spanish Inquisition was established precisely at that time to ensure Christian orthodoxy and stamp out heresy and apostasy.

Columbus shared this religious passion with his sponsors, especially the pious Queen Isabel. He promised to turn over much of what he stood to earn by his voyages to the Queen and the Church for the restoration of Christianity in the Holy Land and to crush the infidels. These were grandiose visions when one considers the boundaries of the world inhabited by Columbus, until one recalls that in his commercial voyages in the service of Portugal, he already had reached probably as far north as Iceland and had visited the African coast far to the south before taking off on his voyage of discovery in August, 1492. Columbus, the religious zealot, was also Columbus the merchant and experienced explorer. Other events also drove Europeans farther into the Atlantic world.

When in 1453 Constantinople fell to the Turkish Ottomans, the orientation of European trade shifted from the Mediterranean to the Atlantic, with Portugal leading the way down the African coast and into the Atlantic islands. The profitable trade in African slaves grew as Portuguese explorers pushed down the coast of West Africa, while other trade between Portugal and Africa was equally lucrative. Horses, saddles, stirrups, cloth, caps, hats, saffron, wine, wheat, salt, lead, iron, steel, copper, and brass all moved south and east from Portugal to be traded for African slaves, gold, animal skins, gum arabic, cotton, malagueta pepper, parrots, and even camels. It remained for the visionary Columbus to challenge the Portuguese crawl down around Africa on their way to Asia by proposing to sail directly west across the Ocean Sea (the Atlantic) to reach the East. That was his Great Enterprise that he had presented to Isabel and Ferdinand as early as the 1480s, but only received his commission and their blessing after the fall of Granada.

Columbus had actually presented the idea to the Portuguese court earlier, but a learned and experienced commission appointed by the King rejected both Columbus's premise and his plan. The commission said he had grossly underestimated the actual circumference of the globe and that the voyage he was proposing—from the Atlantic coast of the Iberian

Figure 1.1   Painting (Detail) from 1882: Boabdil confronted by Ferdinand and Isabel after the Fall of Granada, 1492. The capture of Granada in 1492 completed the Reconquest of Spain for Christendom. Here King Ferdinand of Aragón and his wife, Queen Isabel of Castile, receive the surrender of Muhammad XII, Abu 'abd-Allah Muhammad XII (1460–1533), known as Boabdil (a Spanish corruption of the name *Abu Abdullah*).

peninsula to the islands off the Chinese coast—was impossible given the distance and time that would have to be spent at sea. It could not be done. And the commission was right on both counts. What neither the commission nor Columbus accounted for was the existence of the American continents about 3000 miles to the west, blocking the passage to the East.

The Portuguese continued to explore down the coast of Africa, looking for a way to round that continent and then sail to India, for the capture of Constantinople earlier in the century by the Turks had made the search for alternate lines of trade to the great emporiums of Asia even more urgent for European merchants long dependent upon the overland route to India and the East.

Over the next several decades Seville, the quiet medieval port of the province of Andalucia, was rapidly transformed into the entrepôt of

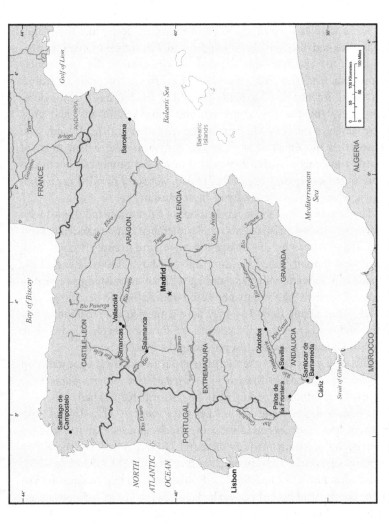

Map 1.1 The Iberian peninsula, showing Spain and Portugal and many of the cities and provinces where Las Casas lived and worked.

seaborne traffic with the Indies. While some of the early fleets to the Indies sailed from ports along the Atlantic coast—Cádiz, Huelva, Sanlúcar de Barrameda, for example—after the turn of the century, Seville was more and more preferred for assembly and dispatch of the fleets.

These were exciting times. News of returning fleets from the islands Columbus had discovered commingled with the decrees of new crusades. In 1500, for example, the Muslims of Granada, under increasingly oppressive Christian rule, revolted. The primate of Spain, Cardinal Francisco Jiménez de Cisneros (1436–1517), wanted more conversions, less heresy (by the new converts), and more conformity, and grew increasingly intolerant. He was backed by Isabel and Ferdinand, who sensed that the Muslims of Granada, and to a lesser extent those of Castile and Aragón, where they existed in smaller numbers, nonetheless represented a suspicious minority. If Spain were ever invaded again from Africa, where would the loyalty of these Muslims lie?

The Muslims of Granada rebelled out of frustration and disgust with the perfidy of the Christians who spoke tolerance, but demanded conversion. The campaigns of subjugation were brutal and effective. King Ferdinand himself joined the campaign in March, 1500, slaying all the inhabitants in some villages, claiming with an astonishing satisfaction that in Lanjerón "the occupants were baptized before perishing."[4] Las Casas—then about 15 or 16—may have witnessed the rebellion at first hand and perhaps even marched with militia from Seville dispatched in 1500 to Granada to assist in suppressing the Muslim rebels.

Fifty-five years later, when writing about the physical appearance of the city of Tlaxcala in Mexico in his *Apologética Historia Sumaria* (a treatise on the Indians of America), he remembered Granada.

"From a distance and below," Las Casas wrote, "Tlascala looks like nothing less than Granada, in Spain, which appears that way coming from Archidona if my memory serves me because it has been more than fifty-five years since I saw so much of that city, like the Alhambra, which is the royal house."[5] More than likely, his overland trip to Granada was in the company of his father, who had returned from the Indies two years earlier, in 1498. Being merchants, they may have been only lightly armed and witnessed nothing more than an uneasy province, cold glances from Moorish villagers, and mounted Christian knights thundering by on veteran war horses.

If by 1500 Columbus was a seasoned explorer, navigator, and governor of Spain's growing claims on the islands he discovered, the young Las Casas was just beginning his career. He was bright, curious, and energetic, and probably already possessed the quick temper he became so famous for. He had studied Latin and theology with his uncle in the Cathedral school in Seville and was an apt learner. He could size up situations and people rapidly, had a rather good opinion of himself, and did not suffer from a lack of confidence. In addition to abundant energy and a penetrating mind, he possessed a phenomenal physical endurance. He certainly needed the latter just to survive the eight trans-Atlantic voyages he made during his lifetime where the water was foul, the food wormy, the company close, and sea sickness the incessant companion of the landsman.

We come away with the image of a self-confident teenager of 15 or 16 in 1500, cocky to the point of brash. "Bold to the point of temerity, sharp-witted and eloquent ... he was always to command respect, though in the case of his numerous enemies this was sometimes mingled with fear."[6]

The coming and going of ships and fleets quickened as the century neared an end, and the return of his father in 1498 from Santo Domingo pointed him in the direction of the Indies. His father had returned to Seville on a small fleet that sailed from Santo Domingo on October 18, 1498. Three hundred Taino Indian slaves also traveled on those ships. One of them, renamed Juanico, was given to Las Casas by his father who had received Juanico as a gift from the Admiral—Columbus himself. In fact, Columbus had given slaves to each of the Spaniards returning from the islands. When the Queen, then in Seville, heard the news, she exploded in anger.

"What right does the Admiral have to give my vassals to anyone?" she asked indignantly, and rhetorically. Isabel, of course, was in a position not only to question such impertinence on the part of the Admiral, but also to take action. She ordered all the Indians returned to their homes in Santo Domingo, "on pain of death" as Las Casas recalled many years later while composing his history of the Conquest. Las Casas was surprised at the severity of her reaction.[7]

"I don't know why the Queen so angrily and emphatically demanded that these three hundred Indians which the Admiral had enslaved be returned, especially when she'd said nothing about others the Admiral had sent."[8] Las Casas could not think of no other "reason, other than perhaps the Queen thought that the previous Indians brought over had been enslaved in a just war."[9] Whatever he may have thought, his new Indian friend Juanico was returned in the June, 1500 fleet to Santo Domingo commanded by Francisco de Bobadilla. This famous knight commander who had served the Queen in the recent wars against the Muslims was sent to investigate charges of mismanagement and corruption leveled against Columbus by Spanish settlers on the island.

Bobadilla's fleet arrived in the harbor of Santo Domingo on August 23, 1500. While he waited for the tide to change to enter the harbor, he was shocked to see seven corpses swinging from the gallows. Going ashore, the knight commander discovered five more Castilians waiting to swing, sentenced to death by Columbus for insurrection and treason. Bobadilla did not tarry very long to investigate the matter, one that had been simmering between Columbus and the Spanish-born settlers who resented the Genoese mariner for his high-handed ways. The Admiral of the Ocean Sea was arrested and shackled. Bobadilla returned him to Spain on a small fleet that sailed in October, 1500. The master of the ship offered to release the Admiral for the long voyage, but Columbus refused. The Queen and King would have to face him in his ignoble state and, hopefully, be shamed by his condition. It worked.

Soon after he came ashore at Cádiz in November, the sovereigns ordered his chains struck and commanded that Columbus travel to the court then in Granada. Las Casas witnessed much of this. He not only recalled that the King and Queen sent Columbus a generous allowance—two thousand ducats—to make the trip to Granada, but also recounted the details of Columbus's dramatic appearance at court with an eye-witness's ring of authenticity.

Las Casas must have been in the city of Granada when Columbus presented himself—the injured martyr, unjustly jailed, abused in language and body—before the King and Queen for justice. The scene is one of the most remarkable in the age of exploration. The Queen was especially compassionate and loving. Ferdinand joined with his wife in expressing sorrow at the unfortunate turn of events, but "in truth, she always favored and defended him [Columbus] more than the King," remarked Las Casas.[10] Once Columbus was exonerated and in the good graces of his sovereigns again, he made one last voyage—his fourth—to the New World in 1502.

While Columbus was fully vindicated by Isabel and Ferdinand, Bobadilla, on the other hand, was never punished for arresting Columbus and returning him to Spain in chains so ignominiously. Instead he drowned in a massive storm in late June, 1502, when his fleet was caught by a hurricane just as they sailed from Santo Domingo bound for Spain.

In 1500 and 1501, Las Casas criss-crossed the mountainous kingdom of Granada with his father, traveling as merchants. When Isabel and Ferdinand contracted with Nicolás de Ovando on September 3, 1501, in Granada to replace Governor Bobadilla, the Las Casas, father and son, were there. Las Casas's father Pedro signed on with Ovando's expedition. Ovando, a Cistercian friar with long experience fighting Muslims in the Queen's armies, put together a fleet of 32 vessels in Seville and dropped down the River Guadalquivir early in February to rendezvous at Sanlúcar de Barrameda at the mouth of the river. Some 2500 men, many of them nobles, gentlemen, and principal people, made up the expedition. Included were 12 Franciscan friars. The fleet sailed for Santo Domingo from Sanlúcar on February 13, 1502. Las Casas was on board Ovando's fleet which arrived off the coast of Santo Domingo on April 15 after a voyage of two months.

Ovando was dispatched by Isabel and Ferdinand to replace Bobadilla because Columbus had complained so bitterly of the injustices and injuries to his command and his person. The Spanish sovereigns, always sympathetic to their Admiral of the Ocean Sea, appointed Ovando, a member of the military order of Alcántara, and a proven leader. While Columbus was the leading edge of Spain's explosive burst into the Americas, Ovando governed Santo Domingo for the next eight years and set the tone for the establishment of royal government in Spain's New World colonies. The pattern for the exploration and conquest of the Americas was being set.

Following the "discovery" of the New World by Columbus there came the other explorers and conquistadors, often one and the same. The conquistadors swept over the islands—Española [modern Dominican Republic and Haiti], followed by Puerto Rico and then Cuba—and over the next half century they gradually mapped the dimensions of the New

World, beginning with the islands of the Caribbean and, after "reducing" the Amerindians to obedience, went on to explore and conquer great portions of the mainland: North America, Central America, and South America.

Modern interpretations

In modern interpretations, sharply different points of view have emerged about this unique moment in history, when peoples from two different worlds—those from the Eurasian and African continents (largely the Spaniards and Portuguese in these early stages) and those in the Americas—first came into contact. As noted in the Introduction, the Spanish called this era the Conquest. The "Encounter" has been substituted in modern times to emphasize not the dominance of one culture over another, but the meeting of different cultures without necessarily assigning superiority of one over another. "Contact" period has also been applied to the early period of exploration and discovery, for similar reasons. After all, the Amerindians were not "lost," nor in fact "discovered" except from a very narrow European point of view, expressing "Eurocentrism." And some of the severest critics of the Conquest/Encounter have substituted "invasion" as a descriptor of the era, as in the Invasion of America. In this scenario, Amerindian culture was disrupted and destroyed by invading Europeans, much as the barbarians—Huns, Goths, Celts—invaded and finally destroyed the Roman Empire.

While we need to be aware of the new labels, we need not get lost in a semantic labyrinth. One of the principal reasons for much of the newer interpretations or labeling was to recover the voice of the Amerindians, lost in the traditional literature of the Encounter/Conquest, which was largely generated, of course, by Spanish chroniclers and historians themselves. Ironically the one major source for the voice of the "other," another label to describe peoples or classes of people who traditionally did not keep written records, was Las Casas himself. We shall revisit these issues below. In 1502, he was still a young man on his first voyage to the New World and the wonder of it no doubt transfixed him as it did many voyagers after a long crossing of the high seas.

As one nears land, life quickens aboard any ship. The first land one sees after crossing the Atlantic in these equatorial latitudes are the Windward Islands, which stretch in a great semi-circle to the north and west from the coast of South America to the larger islands of Puerto Rico and Española. At a distance, the Windward Islands first appear on the horizon as dark brown smudges, not very different from low-lying clouds. From previous voyages, the sailors knew the islands appeared 40 or 50 days from the Canaries. Names were attached to specific islands, many bestowed by Columbus himself.

On his third voyage, 1498–1500, Columbus had discovered the mainland of South America. He skirted and named the island of Trinidad in honor of the Holy Trinity, and sailed past the mouth of the mighty Orinoco River, its fresh water flowing far out to sea. From this fact Columbus speculated that he might be near the Earthly Paradise, for it was thought to be the source of the four greatest rivers in the world, the Ganges, Tigris, Euphrates, and Nile. Writing almost three decades later, Las Casas gently chided the naïveté of the Admiral, based on a rather skimpy knowledge of Scripture and much conjecture. But Columbus may have had other reasons to speculate, and here we can see through Las Casas's eyes as Columbus approached the islands for the first time.

"That the admiral thought he may be nearing the terrestrial paradise is not without some good reason," Las Casas wrote, "especially when one considers the soft, gentle breezes, the fresh, green beauty of the trees, and the joyful quality of the land."

"Each part and parcel of the land seems like paradise," Las Casas remembered, as he recreated, in his mind's eye, the end of a long sea voyage.[11]

His small ship plowed on through, as she had for weeks in the monotonous rhythm of the crossing, in and out of deep blue waves. After five or six weeks, everyone was looking for signs of land. Las Casas recalled his first view of the islands, the brown smudges slowly giving way to the rich, deep greens of tropical forests, high mountains, some volcanic, rising from beneath the sea. They passed by some of the islands of the Windward chain already named by Columbus, *Maria Galante, Dominica, Guadalupe.* Many still preserve the same names today.

Then the fleet turned north once in the Caribbean and headed for the large island of Española. Instead of ocean all around them and small

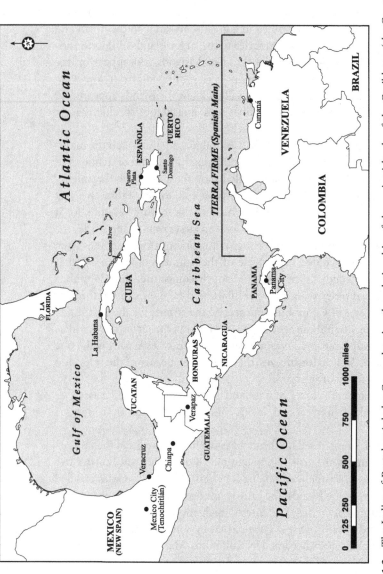

Map 1.2 The Indies of Bartolomé de las Casas, showing the relationship of the major islands of the Caribbean (the Greater Antilles) and the Viceroyalties of New Spain (Mexico and Central America) and of Peru. Source: Ramón Menéndez Pidal, *El padre las Casas, su doble personalidad* (Madrid: Espasa-Calipe, S. A., 1963), map between pp. 40–41 which appeared originally in a book by same author, *Imagen del mundo hacia 1570* (1944), on p. 87 as "Los virreinos y audiencias." His map in *El padre*

islands passing by, land occupies their starboard [right] side for as far as they can see as they approach the port of Santo Domingo from the south and east.

The chatter of the crew increases, lowering sails, making ready to let go the anchor, preparing for the arrival. With a full tide the ships slip into the harbor of Santo Domingo, the verdant colors of the tropics, the smells of anchorage and quayside, redolent of tropical plants, spiced with the pungent effluvia of human occupation, all brighten a weary traveler's senses. It is an arrival by sea; it is like no other. It means a connection hås been made. Las Casas made many over his long career.

Conquest of La Española

But the island paradise which he thought he arrived at was in fact being turned into a living hell by his fellow countrymen. Las Casas lived on the island for the next ten years and witnessed the brutal treatment and exploitation of the Taino people by the Spanish settlers.

Las Casas later recorded what he witnessed in those ten years and that account appeared in his little book, *A Brief History of the Destruction of the Indies* (1552). From *A Brief History* the Black Legend was spun, portraying the Spanish as uniquely cruel and barbaric in the conquest and settlement of the Americas, and it has developed into one of the most controversial of the many *puntos de vista*, or viewpoints, covered in this series of books.

As the Introduction noted, the Black Legend is at the center of one of the major historiographical issues of the Encounter, and, indeed, of western civilization: were the Spanish indeed uniquely cruel and barbaric in their encounter and conquest of Amerindians, or were they simply behaving in a norm that reflected current values and practices across the European world of the epoch? Las Casas's eyewitness account is both powerful and heartrending. It is one of the best examples of the power and immediacy, not to speak of authenticity, of the eye witness, of original documentation in the study and interpretation of the past.

The competing theory that arose to counter the Black Legend—the White Legend—tends to whitewash the Spanish behavior as nothing more than a people acting within the norms and principles of the time.

Later arrivals to the Americas—the English, French, and Dutch, for example—were themselves equally guilty of devastating and diminishing the Amerindians. Las Casas's arrival at Santo Domingo, however, was not concerned with the stuff of legends and history, but with the excitement of a young man finally reaching port after a long sea voyage.[12]

No sooner had Las Casas's ship arrived in the harbor of Santo Domingo than the excited inhabitants tumbled out from shore in boats and crowded around the ships shouting questions. "What's the news? Who is coming to govern?"

"Good news!" shouted the passengers, leaning over, watching the sailors lower the ship's own boats. "The Queen and King send us the gentleman of Lares [Nicolas de Ovando] of the Order of Alcántara, and all is well at home."

Usually the next question is "What's happening here?"[13]

"Great news! Lots of gold to be found! Huge nuggets! And just the other day the Indians rebelled! We've already captured hundreds and enslaved them." That meant more Indians to work the mines, more Indians to be returned to Castile to be sold as slaves.

Gold fever infected the new arrivals. Loading their backpacks they set off like an army of ants for the mines. Those without servants carried their tools with them. Greed had an equalizing effect even on this rigid old medieval society now newly transferred to the islands of the New World.

Gentleman and craftsmen, grandfathers and teenagers, they all worked like men possessed, Las Casas later recalled in his *History*. Digging and eating, digging and eating, until they finally ran out of their stale food and gave up, returning to Santo Domingo, really still no more than a village, and poor itself. Hungry, disillusioned, and feverish, they died by the hundreds that first month. More than a thousand perished, so fast that the few priests could barely keep up with the burials. Las Casas watched—and later recorded—it all in astonishment. He noticed that the few Spaniards devoted to a semblance of farming and pig herding made out quite well in this hothouse of overheated expectations, easy gold (for some at any rate), and outrageous prices, especially for food.

Some on the fleet had brought with them a large supply of merchandise such as clothes and tools, and they made small fortunes, especially among the inhabitants who had gold, but whose clothes were in tatters. Provisioning the incoming settlers and the outgoing fleets produced a decent living for Las Casas's father, Pedro. Young Las Casas was soon also farming land given to his family by Columbus, as well as moving around the island acquiring provisions to sell to outgoing fleets.

"It's almost a rule around these parts," Las Casas wrote, "that all those given to mining were always in need, and even in debtors' jail."

"On the other hand, those given to farming and ranching were much better off."[14]

Earliest relations between Spaniards and Tainos were mixed. In the very early period, or the interregnum between Columbus's first voyage and the arrival of Las Casas on the island in 1502, both invaders and residents co-habited and mixed as much as they fought and competed.[15] It was by no means idyllic, but the sexual overtures of the early Spaniards for example were received quite well by the Tainos, who gave the first visitors—sailors in Columbus's fleet—women to celebrate the visit of such important personages. The aggressive Spaniards figured this habit was shared by all Tainos and proceeded to take more women, many against their will. The upshot was the massacre of those Spaniards which Columbus left behind in 1493 in a tiny settlement named La Navidad when he returned to Spain after his first voyage.

When Columbus returned in his second voyage in late 1493, all the Spaniards were gone. He quickly ascertained that the lust for women and gold had provoked the first Indian "uprising" in the Americas, although in truth it was not an uprising or revolt. It was simply a defiant expression of Taino independence and unwillingness to submit to such blatant avarice and covetousness.

By the time Las Casas arrived, some Tainos, especially women, had adapted to the Spanish presence, entered into unions with them—inside or outside the boundaries of marriage—and the first generation of *mestizos* came into existence, part Spaniard, part Taino, the genesis of a new people. Las Casas had reason later in his life to encourage these relations between Spaniards and Indians as a means of overcoming the distance growing between conquistador/invaders and the Amerindians of the recipient cultures.

But even as Spaniards and Tainos had relations—forced or otherwise— and thus forged the beginnings of a new civilization in the Americas, many of the conquistador/settlers imposed themselves on the simple Tainos with shocking barbarity.

In a story recounted by Las Casas, some Spanish settlers—armed with swords and accompanied by their war dogs—went to the island of Saona to get provisions. The dogs were "fierce beasts, trained to tear apart Indians, who rightly feared them more than their own devils."[16] The Tainos on the island made haste to load the boat to transport the cassava bread to the caravel. They were urged on by their *cacique*, or local leader, who encouraged them to work rapidly for the Spaniards.

One of the Spaniards had a dog on a leash. The dog watched the *cacique* moving his staff up and down as he encouraged his people to work faster to please the Spaniards. The dog growled and pulled hard on the leash wanting to get at the Indian. His master was having trouble controlling him.

He said to a companion, "Hey, I wonder what would happen if we let the dog loose?"

Thinking they could restrain him, the two Spaniards yelled, "Sic 'em," in jest, thinking they could hold the dog.

The dog went wild upon hearing the command and lunged at the *cacique*, dragging the Spaniard who finally had to let go of the leash. The dog struck the Indian in the stomach and tore out his entrails. Mortally wounded, the Indian fled holding his guts as the dog played with the bloody prize.

Hearing of this outrage, a *cacique* named Cotubanamá from the nearby province of Higuey swore revenge and shortly thereafter the Tainos ambushed and killed a party of eight Spaniards who had gone ashore during another voyage.

Las Casas thought the eight deserved to die, even if they were not among those who had allowed their dog to disembowel the Taino earlier. The Indians were rendering justice and they could, and should, hold Spaniards accountable. A sympathy for, and ability to see the Indian point of view, became an early hallmark of Las Casas as he recorded many examples of brutal exploitation on the island that he witnessed over the next ten years.

Las Casas's concern with the "other," or the voices of those in history traditionally without a voice, emerges in this period. Since history is mostly based on written documents, the "other" has to be "heard" by alterative means: oral records, testimony of sympathetic observers (such as Las Casas obviously), by a sophisticated analysis of language and the symbolism of words and phrases (semiotics) to discover the "voices" of the other. Perhaps the other was an Indian culture (such as the Taino) which had no written language. Or the other could be slaves not permitted to learn to read and write. Or, in a society that kept women largely away from learning, the other could be women, especially the vast majority in the peasant and lower classes. Yet, the growing compassion and sympathy of Las Casas for the Tainos were not the norm. In fact, relations between Spaniards and Tainos had early on begun to harden into the conquerors and the conquered, a distinction that came to characterize early society in Latin America.

Indians who had been enslaved, or those assigned to individual settlers supplied the principal labor for Spaniards. The *encomienda* (which has no proper English translation) was a feudal institution imported into the island by some of Columbus's early settlers from Castile. It resembled the medieval relationship between landlord and peasant. Indians in towns and villages were distributed in *encomienda* to individual Spaniards, the *encomenderos*, who extracted tributary labor (such as working in the mines) from them. The Indians, in turn, were to be protected, civilized, and Christianized by the *encomenderos*.

Another institution, the *repartimiento* (which can be roughly translated as the "distribution" or "apportionment"), was closely associated with the *encomienda*. It too demanded tributary labor, but the resources (the Indians) were usually distributed by royal officials or their representatives. Both institutions evolved closely in the next half century but the bottom line was that Indians were assigned to work for Spaniards, regardless if Indians were assigned to a specific settler, the *encomendero*, or were assigned by the *repartimiento* for specific tasks and at specified times of the year. In each case, both were forms of tributary labor.

The Tainos of Española were distributed in *encomienda* early on by the Spanish governors—Columbus, Bobadilla, Ovando. The *encomienda* became the central instrument of Indian exploitation on the island and it was exported to other islands and finally to the mainland as the Spanish conquest advanced in the next half century. Las Casas soon learned to his horror how Spaniards treated *encomienda* Indians. Over the next several years Las Casas witnessed other atrocities, or heard of them from first hand testimony, which seared his senses and became imbedded in his memory.

Between 1502 and 1506, numerous Spanish expeditions were launched from Santo Domingo across the island to control the Indians. Las Casas went on some of these expeditions; others he heard about. Taken together with the brutal exploitation of forced Taino labor in the gold mines, the experiences formed the basis for his life's work: defending the Indians within his growing understanding of biblical, legal, and ethical principles.

Yet, even amidst the savagery of the first few years of the Spanish occupation of Española, instances of accommodation and adaption were not unusual. The Tainos, and later other Indian peoples across the Americas, first resisted and then accommodated themselves to the Spanish invasion as it swept across the Caribbean islands, and then spilled onto the mainland and into the heart of great Amerindian empires, such as that of the Aztec in Mexico and the Inca in Peru. But in those later instances of the Conquest, the Indian populations numbered in the tens of millions and the sheer size of the populations buffered the devastating effects of the Spanish invasion, especially as European epidemic diseases spread among an Amerindian population which had no immunities to these diseases new to the Americas.

There still exists (and always will, given the paucity of evidence) different interpretations and points of view on the actual effects of diseases on the process of the Conquest. Without a demographic baseline (the actual size of the population of the Americas at the commencement of European contact, for example), it is hard to determine the extent of dislocation and death that entered with European diseases such as measles, bubonic and pneumonic plague, typhus, and smallpox.[17] That Indian populations were devastated is true. By the middle of the sixteenth century, there were virtually no Tainos left on Española. And "General Smallpox" is generally credited with giving Hernán Cortés a hand in defeating the Aztecs in 1521. While the experience of Spaniards and Tainos on the island of Española was not exactly replicated by the rest of the encounter between Europeans and Amerindians across the Americas, it did prefigure in a significant way the refashioning of life.

Las Casas traveled widely through the island between 1502 and 1509. He ate and stayed with the Tainos occasionally and observed, rather sarcastically, that they were not, as rival historian Gonzalo Fernández de Oviedo wrote, savages living in caves, but rather they lived in villages and towns and were governed as any other civilized people. They worked their fields and gardens like any other farmers.[18]

Las Casas also witnessed many scenes of brutality and savagery. Swords slashing through Taino bone and flesh, the splash of blood, the boasts and boots of the Spaniards; those images were burned into his life forever. The blood-spattered rocks and trails where the Indians sought to escape, the pleas for help, the innocent being slaughtered, these and other scenes run through his writings like an awful refrain.

Some battles lasted all day and into the night, the Tainos fleeing their villages into the mountains and forests where they had hidden the women and children. The Spanish invariably pursued them, determined to capture the chiefs and *caciques*, and make examples of them. No matter how stealthily and quietly the Tainos made their way through the forests, the Spaniards followed the trails. Catching one Indian, they would torture him for information. Catching groups of cowering natives, they would put them to the sword—men, women, and children—to terrify and terrorize the rest into submission.[19]

"The Spaniards bragged about their various cruelties, each trying to top the others on novel ways to spill blood," Las Casas recorded.[20]

Three Tainos were tied together and slowly strangled "in honor of Christ, our Redeemer, and of his twelve Apostles." Before dying, the Spaniards tried out their cutting skills, some showing off their reverse strokes, opening the Tainos from chest to groin, their entrails spilling out. Some, still alive, were then thrown into pits and burned. Two small boys, no more than two years old, were stabbed through the throat and cut open, and then thrown from the cliffs.

"I saw all this, and more, so foreign to human nature. I shudder to tell it. Perhaps it was a nightmare. I can hardly believe it myself," Las Casas wrote sadly. "Even though other cruelties were perpetrated in these Indies, some worse and infinitely larger, I don't think I will ever forget these." He never did.

The island was "pacified, if 'pacified' we can in truth call it," Las Casas wrote with bitter sarcasm, "seeing as how the Spaniards were at war with God, free now to oppress these people with great liberty, and nobody, great or small, to resist them." Las Casas wrote of these atrocities in the mid-1520s. The native population had been decimated by then, so that those who arrived at the island asked if the Indians there were whites or blacks, referring to the growing African slave presence.[21]

This was a very fluid period in the relations between Europeans and Indians. When 18-year-old Las Casas landed in the Indies in 1502, few laws or regulations existed for governing the Indians or the Indies. It was natural that Governor Ovando establish some firm, recognizable order. Those, in fact, were his instructions, and Isabel and Ferdinand expected him to comply. In doing so, he set the pattern for the future conquest and settlement of the Americas.

In a chapter of his *History* entitled "The Creation of the *Encomienda*," Las Casas described in detail how Ovando organized the Tainos to labor for the Spaniards. It is one of the most biting passages in Las Casas's writings, filled with ridicule when he is not lamenting the tragedy.[22] In theory, the Spanish were to instruct, indoctrinate, and convert the Indians. Las Casas recorded his own view of what in fact Governor Ovando did in this area. "In the nine years of his government of this island, he was no more interested in the indoctrination and salvation of the Indians than if they were sticks and stones, or cats and dogs."

Las Casas's record of events on the island reads like a legal indictment. Who did Ovando put to work? Men certainly, but he also ordered children and old people, nursing women and pregnant women, chiefs and common people and the very lords and natural kings of the towns and lands, into the mines and fields of the Spaniards. "This distribution among the Spaniards of the Indians was called the '*repartimiento*.'"[23] In this way, all the Tainos were distributed to the Spaniards, "condemned to service forever where, in the end, they died. This was the liberty which the *repartimiento* secured."

Men were forced to work 10, 20, 30, 40, and even 80 leagues away from their homes in the mining of gold. Exhausted from these labors, beaten down and starving, the men returned to their homes unable to consummate their marriages. In this manner, a generation was lost and never replaced. Babies were born puny and tiny and perished for lack of milk. The women, overworked and underfed, dried up. Some mothers drowned their babies out of desperation. Others, pregnant, took herbs to abort and cut short their pregnancies.

The Spanish overseers used whips and canes to keep the pace up, berating the Indians as "dogs." Those poor souls who escaped the hell were chased down and returned. Some Spaniards were designated *visitadores*, or inspectors, by Ovando and put in charge of villages. They were given an extra 100 Tainos in addition to their original *encomiendas*. When escaped Tainos were returned, they had to stand judgment before the *visitador*.

The trial and punishment were swift and cruel. Tied to a post, they were whipped with a lash dipped in tar. The famished, thin Tainos were lashed to a bloody pulp and usually left for dead. "I saw this many times with my own eyes," Las Casas later recorded. "And God is my witness that many fell on those poor lambs ..." The metaphorical substitution of lambs for Indians clearly showed how Las Casas viewed these victims, for lambs were often the sacrificial animals of the Old Testament. In the New Testament, Jesus himself assumed the role of the lamb of God who sacrificed himself to atone for the sins of man. Jesus, conversely, is sometimes portrayed as the shepherd, a tender, loving guardian of the flock. What of these Spanish shepherds on the island? Las Casas disabused the reader of any notion that they were shepherds in the Scriptural sense, but more like wolves who prey on the flock. In each instance, a metaphor for the predator, rather than the guardian, is drawn by Las Casas.

Las Casas pounded away in his indictment of Spanish behavior. The Spanish were contemptuous of the Indians, treating them worse than the beasts of the field. His comparisons are direct, his language unforgiving. "And even the beasts usually have some liberty to go graze in the pastures, a liberty which our Spaniards denied the poor miserable Indians. And so, in truth, they were in perpetual slavery, for they were deprived of their free will to do but like beasts whose owners keep them tethered."

To do this to human beings was contemptible.

When the famished and sickly Indians could no longer work, they were allowed to go home. "The poor souls went, usually falling into the first ravines, dying from desperation. A few made it to their homes. And I came upon some of the dead on the roads, and others under the trees, gasping; and others groaning in the pain of death. A few saying 'Hungry! Hungry!'"[24]

To escape the hunger and pain, many chose suicide, drinking the poisonous juice from the cassava plant. "This was the liberty and good treatment and Christianity given these people by the *Comendador Mayor* [Governor Ovando]."[25] The governor was held strictly accountable by Las Casas, for while governors and viceroys were held in high esteem, much was expected from them as well. The prophetic nature of Las Casas's character rises and is clearly evident.

A wrong, a terrible injustice, had been perpetrated and Ovando did not intervene to stop it. His guilt was incontrovertible to Las Casas. Ovando was guilty not only before man, but also before God. "Before God," Las Casas wrote "because throwing rational, free men into such a cruel and hellish captivity constituted an evil and went against divine and natural law, even more so when experience showed clearly what was happening." Las Casas recounted horror after horror, sometimes repeating himself, to drive home the message.

The scenes that unfolded before his eyes (so at odds with the teachings of Jesus Christ), led to a decision he eventually had to make as a Christian: to take up the cause of the Indians and so to enter through the small gate and take the straight and narrow road to life, salvation, and justice, or pass through the wide gate and follow the broad road to destruction.

2

Justice for All

As early as 1503 and 1504, Las Casas sensed that this emerging order was seriously flawed. He was shocked at the brutality and callousness of the Spaniards. Burning heretics and catapulting Muslim body parts into besieged cities may have been common practice at home for Christian warriors of his era during the final stages of the Reconquest, but these innocent people were not Muslim apostates and heretics.

To force the Tainos to work, Ovando told the sovereigns that the natives were escaping and fleeing work and needed to be brought to heel. A day's work would be rewarded with a day's pay, a *jornal*. But, Ovando wrote, even with this great inducement, the Indians ran away to avoid serving the Spaniards. "Lies! Lies!" countered Las Casas. The Tainos in fact were fleeing from the oppression and tyranny inflicted by the Spaniards. The Tainos ran away "like chicks and small birds fleeing hawks," not because of some desire to be disobedient but to survive this onslaught. Besides, after what the Spaniards had done to them, the Indians would rather deal with tigers than the "Christians."[1]

Las Casas asked rhetorically what Indians in their right minds would leave their homes, their women, and their children and travel 50 and 100 leagues to work for the Spaniards, even if they paid them a daily wage? Were not the campaigns waged by the Admiral [Columbus] and other governors calculated to bring the Indians into slavery and servitude? Who was gaining when ships were sent to Castile full of Taino slaves?

Bartolomé de las Casas and the Conquest of the Americas. Lawrence A. Clayton
© 2011 Lawrence A. Clayton

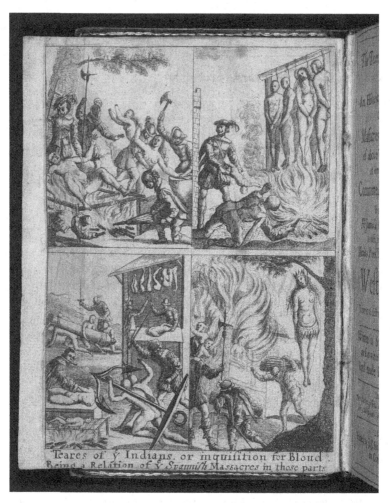

Figure 2.1 The Black Legend, graphically depicted by Protestants, helped fuel anti-Spanish sentiments among Spain's European rivals, especially England, Holland, and France. Based on Las Casas's writings, this account is entitled "*The Tears of the Indians: Being an historical and true account of the cruel massacres and slaughters of above twenty millions of innocent people; committed by the Spaniards …*" This account was published in England in the mid-seventeenth century.

"There's not a man in his right mind who would come to work for the Spaniards for a day's wage under those circumstances. They are even LESS compelled by natural or divine law," Las Casas added.

Defenders of Ovando and the ongoing "pacification" of the Tainos contended that they needed to bring the Indians together to teach them the Holy Catholic Faith. To this Las Casas erupted in sarcastic humor. "I can attest that neither then nor in subsequent years was there any more effort to bring Christianity to these people than there was to teach the Faith to the mares and horses and other beasts of the field." Las Casas's rival chronicler Oviedo defended Ovando's point of view by claiming there was no one to help Spaniards mine for gold, till the fields, to plant and harvest, and build the sinews of the new colony.

Putting himself in the place of the Indians, Las Casas answered as they might have.

"If you want fields to bear, work them yourselves."

"If you want to get rich on gold, pick up the tools and dig yourself."

"We are not the vagabonds, idlers, and loafers around here. We eat only from the sweat of our hands and complied a lot better than the Spaniards with the second precept which God gave men."[2] Las Casas summarized his reasoning—apart from the obvious—to support his views. In no way were the Indians compelled to contribute "even one *maravedí*" to the Spaniards.[3]

Las Casas invoked reason, natural law, positive divine law, and human laws to affirm his position and said even the simplest human being could understand this. He did not simply argue against the abuses and outrageous behavior of the conquistador/*encomendero* class. Cruelty and torture were, after all, a part of life in the sixteenth century, not necessarily excusable by modern standards, but certainly explainable by those standards that governed in the past. On the other hand, at the heart of Las Casas's argument is that the Spaniards were committing illegal acts. If this were proven true, the justification for the conquest could be challenged and, indeed, negated.

Later in his life, to undermine the claims of the conquistadors, Las Casas constructed his theoretical, juridical, and theological defense of the Indians. But early in his life he was already chewing on some of the rationalizations thrown up by the Spaniards for their actions. One of these was that to Christianize the pagan Indians, they first had to be brought under authority and taught to obey.

In his *Book of Prophecies* which he compiled in 1501, Christopher Columbus argued that the overriding mission of his great "Enterprise of the Indies" was to fulfill the Great Commission.[4] Columbus dug through the prophetic literature in the Bible and found many passages which he interpreted as predicting his voyage and its consequences. By bringing the pagan peoples of the islands and lands of the New World into the bosom of Christianity, the door was opening for the Second Coming of Christ and the Millennial Kingdom of God's reign on earth. Perhaps it all sounds a little farfetched, and far too mystical, for the modern reader, but contemporaries of Columbus and Las Casas were firmly embedded in historical Christianity and how their lives were ordered in the light of Scripture. It was complicated by many possible interpretations.

Did the right, indeed the responsibility, of conversion imply you could use force, for example? Not brute force, but, at the very least, the removal of impediments to preaching the Word? St. Augustine seemed to have come down on this side of this argument; St. Thomas Aquinas did not. The weight of Scripture clearly did not condone force. So, Las Casas reasoned, the forceful conversion of Indians—even to save them from eternal perdition—was itself an error and contradicted Scripture. Jesus, after all, came in peace. The apostle Paul, who preached to the Gentiles and in many ways was a model for Las Casas, did not use force. If man was by nature free, and possessed a free will to determine right and wrong, then he must be given the choice, not forced. Las Casas later visited these issues in his works in detail and with great erudition.

Las Casas's developing ability to relate to Indian peoples in a compassionate fashion also put him at odds with most of his contemporaries. He entered into the experience of the Indians and looked at the world and what was coming at them with sympathy and understanding. That he could not fully embrace nor wholly articulate their world view is a given. Las Casas was, after all a Spaniard, a European, a Christian, and representative—no matter how much he would deny it—of a European imperialism in the making.[5] He was acting on a stage that was new to them all—Europeans and Indians alike—and he acted, as was natural, from within his own world view and culture.

Discovering his calling

Between 1511 and 1514, Las Casas moved into a new dimension of his life, motivated by compassion and Scripture. The journey was a wrenching one for him personally. In the larger context, his experiences were among the earliest and most important in the spiritual conquest of the New World, or the Christianization of the Americas by Europeans, driven by the Christians' desire to evangelize and convert the Amerindians so they too would be saved within the Christian cosmology.

On the other hand, Amerindians possessed their own well-articulated religions, and for the most part were forced to accept the Christian argument as the conquest spread from the Caribbean islands onto the continents of the Americas. Furthermore, the Spanish Catholic message came not only with a few gentle priests and friars, but also rode into the fields and hamlets and cities of Indian civilization with Spanish knights and warriors, banners and swords proclaiming the one true faith. One student of the phenomenon styled the Christianization of the Americas a "spiritual conquest."[6]

There was another battle at stake during the Conquest, and this was the struggle to reconcile the Spanish desire to exploit the Indians and the wealth of the Americas with an equally strong commitment on the part of some truly to convert the Indians to Christianity peacefully. In a larger context, it is the eternal struggle of humankind to reconcile one's cosmological being with one's worldly nature, and put each in harmony with the other. Historiographically, it is one of the most fascinating discourses in the history of the Conquest, for it pits the competing natures of men against each other, one side responding to the desire for self-aggrandizement, wealth, and power in this world, and the other devoted to the concerns of the spiritual world governed by God. Las Casas, too, struggled between his worldly and his spiritual nature.

Although he also held an *encomienda* and kept Indians in semi-bondage, he was a man being transformed. He could not escape the images of his early years on the island, of dead and dying women and children and the brutalization of these innocent souls by his fellow settlers. Nor could he escape his growth as a child of the Church. This

Figure 2.2 Statue of Antonio de Montesinos, Santo Domingo, Dominican Republic. He delivered the sermon in the Christmas season, 1511, that struck the first chord for human rights in the Americas. Available at: http://images.google.com/images?q=image%20antonio%20de%20montesinos&oe=utf-8&rls=org.mozilla:en-US:official&client=firefox-a&um=1&ie=UTF-8&sa=N&hl=en&tab=wi.

growth was considerably accelerated by a small group of three Dominican friars led by Father Pedro de Córdoba who had arrived on the island in September, 1510.[7] Their message delivered in a series of sermons shocked everyone, including Las Casas.

In the meantime, Las Casas was ordained in 1510, becoming the first "new" priest in the Indies, the first Spaniard to be ordained in the Americas. As a churchman, committed to living out the precepts of Christianity, he found his deepening Christian morality contrasting more and more with the reality of brutality, violence, and injustice on the island.

Las Casas recalled that "Divine Providence brought the Dominican Order to this island to bring it out of the darkness."[8] It did not take the Dominicans long to see there was little of the light of the Gospel alive on the island. Two other friars, Antonio Montesinos and Bernardo de Santo Domingo, both well versed in Scripture and proven preachers, accompanied Córdoba from Spain. A well-meaning settler, Pedro de Lumbreras, offered them a small hut of straw behind his corral as shelter. There he gave them cassava bread with a few eggs thrown in occasionally, and, on rare occasions, a fish or two. The friars slept on crude wooden beds with some straw for their bedding.

Then Las Casas injected a very personal note into his narrative of the arrival of the Dominicans. "This same year," he wrote, "… the priest Bartolomé de las Casas, born in Seville, and one of the 'old timers' on the island, sang a new mass, which was the first new mass sung in all these Indies."[9] So in late October or early November, 1510, Las Casas sang the first Mass in the New World by a new priest.

To be a churchman and engaged heavily with secular life was not, however, unusual in this transformational age of the Church. Clerics often played high profile roles in politics, and were very involved in worldly matters. Such involvement often included prostitution to the world, by keeping mistresses, amassing property, venery, and debauched living. The German monk Martin Luther launched the Protestant Reformation in 1517 by posting a document on the Cathedral Church of Wittenburg detailing the errors and sins of the Church, especially targeting the selling of indulgences, or pardons for souls in Purgatory who needed a little nudge from their earthly family and friends to move them on to Heaven.

There was also a powerful reform movement working its way through the Spanish Church, led by such devout friar-statesmen as Cardinal Ximénez de Cisneros. Reformist elements, especially among the Franciscans and Dominicans (and Cardinal Cisneros was himself a Franciscan), recommitted themselves to piety, to obedience, to poverty, and to living the word of Christ. In a fashion, Las Casas was on the cusp between these two worlds warring for the bodies and souls of church-men, one very worldly, and the other deeply spiritual.

Since his arrival on the island in 1502 Las Casas had owned Indian slaves, held Tainos in *encomienda*, mined gold, and operated his farm/ranch/mine on the Yanique River in the interior part of the island called La Vega. In 1510—the same year he became a fully ordained priest—he met Father Córdoba and his Dominican companions. This meeting proved life-changing.

While Las Casas seesawed between the pull of his newly made wealth and the call of his Christian conscience, the Dominicans, after witnessing the shocking relations between Spaniards and Indians, were not unsure of themselves, or at all ambiguous. Something was seriously amiss, and when they identified it, they spoke the truth seeking justice with an intense conviction that shattered the peace.[10]

Father Montesinos' sermon

The Dominicans had prayed, fasted, and meditated around the clock: How were they to awaken the Christian settlers to the terrible errors they were committing? The friars decided to preach sermons and tell the set-tlers exactly where they stood in relation to the Word of God; to tell them what their reward will be for their greed and inhumanity. The three Dominicans were in complete agreement. They selected the best preacher among them, Antonio Montesinos.

The Christmas season, 1511, was upon them. It was agreed that the first sermon should be preached the fourth Sunday of Advent, or just before Christmas itself. The Scriptural reading chosen was John 1:22–23:

> "Finally they [the Pharisees] said, 'Who are you? Give us an answer to take back to those who sent us. What do you say about yourself?'"

"John replied in the words of Isaiah the prophet, 'I am the voice of one calling in the desert, 'Make straight the way for the Lord.'""

The stage was set. So that no one would miss it, everyone was invited, including Governor Diego Columbus, the leading Crown officials, and jurists. Word of this important sermon was delivered to their very homes. A sermon will be preached in the principal church of Santo Domingo, my lords, so went the announcement, and we wanted you to know that much will be said of interest to you, and we much desire your presence.[11] There would no hiding the lamp of life and truth for these Dominicans, and they ignited a controversy that has not ceased to this day. Although not there, Las Casas later recorded it in his *History*, based on notes given him by Fathers Córdoba and/or Montesinos. This is the only record we have of this sermon and the circumstances surrounding it. It was composed and signed by Montesinos.

Montesinos began with some innocuous enough remarks about the season of Advent after reading Scripture from the Book of John. He had prepared well. Both Isaiah and John the Baptist called people to repent to make way for the coming of the Messiah. Without repentance there was no forgiveness. And without forgiveness, the hardhearted were doomed to perdition. The settlers of Española were in danger of eternal damnation if they continued to plague and enslave Indians. They had to be warned.

So, in effect, the first part of the sermon was directed not to evangelizing the Indians, but to identifying sin among the Spaniards. But Montesinos rapidly moved from the Spaniards to speaking about the people they were persecuting.

"There is a sterility of conscience among you on this island," Montesinos continued, "and a blindness in which you live. You are in mortal danger of condemnation, not realizing the grave sins you are committing with such insensitivity. You are immersed in them and dying in them."[12] Montesinos then hit full stride.

"I want you to know that I have come to this pulpit, I who am the voice of Christ on the desert of this island. And you had better pay attention, not just listen, but heed with all your hearts and all your minds. For this will be something you never heard before, the hardest, harshest, most terrifying news you ever expected to hear. This voice says you are in mortal sin. You live and die in sin for the cruelty and tyranny which you inflict on these innocent people."[13]

Montesinos stung his hearers with a series of rhetorical questions indicting their motives and actions. "By what right and by what law do you hold these Indians in such cruel and horrible servitude? By whose authority have you made such detestable war on these people who lived peacefully in their lands? How can you hold them so oppressed and exhausted, without giving them food nor curing their illnesses? They die daily from the work you demand of them. Let me be perfectly clear. You are killing them to get the gold you so crave! And who among you is taking care to teach them about God the creator? Who is baptizing them, leading them to mass, celebrating holidays and Sundays?"

The next questions were the most important asked during the conquest of the Americas: "Are these not men? Do they not have rational souls? Are you not obliged to love them as yourselves! Don't you understand this? Don't you see this? How can you be in such a profound and lethargic sleep? Be assured that in your state you can no more be saved than Moors or Turks who lack and don't want the faith of Jesus Christ."[14]

Rest assured, he told the shocked congregation: without Christianizing their Tainos and providing restitution for all the ills imposed on them, the Spaniards had no hope of salvation and were little less than infidels—moral Moors. Montesinos evidently astounded the hearers with his boldness. Was this their duty? To Christianize non-Christians? Was not that the duty of the clergy? As one prominent student of Las Casas wrote:

> Thus developed the first significant and public clash in America between the zeal for the propagation of the gospel and the greed for gold and silver among Spaniards, who for centuries had been accustomed to an economy based to some extent on war booty wrested from the Moors.[15]

The immediate reaction was shock and outrage. Writing years later, from the vantage point of having launched not a few sermons himself, Las Casas was not beyond some sardonic humor. "He left them dumbfounded," Las Casas remembered. "Some were furious, others were incorrigible, some were saddened, but, as far as I could tell, none were converted."

Montesinos stepped down from the pulpit, head held high, unafraid. No matter how disagreeable, he had told his hearers what God had told him to say. He was, in that instant, a reminder of the prophetic tradition in Judeo-Christian life, a prophet like Isaiah, or Jeremiah, who spoke the truth in the face of hostility and sin.

The congregation was left murmuring. The leading citizens soon gathered at the home of the Governor to deal with this outrageous priest who told them they were bound for hell. He had not only condemned them and the *encomienda* but also spoken treason against the King who had given them the Indians. Governor Diego Columbus—Christopher's son—led the delegation to the modest Dominican monastery—little more than a hut really—and knocked loudly on the door.

"We demand to see the Vicar!" they shouted as the porter opened the door.

Father Pedro de Córdoba appeared.

"We want that priest who preached the sermon."

"No need gentlemen," Córdoba answered quietly. "If your mercies wish something, I will respond for my brothers."

"No! no! We want the priest," the group, hardly more than a high-level mob, demanded.

"No, gentlemen. I am here as the vicar of this Dominican house and you will speak with me, or not at all," Córdoba said, standing his ground.[16]

Columbus and the others began to back down. "We just want to talk with him, Father," they said. "You can be present. We want to know what got into him to preach such a prejudicial sermon, a disservice to the King and damaging to all the citizens of this city and island." Seeing the mob-like atmosphere quiet, Father Córdoba asked Montesinos to join them, having invited the Governor and a few of the leading citizens into the Dominicans' home. They all sat down.

"How did you come to preach such a sermon, Father?" asked Columbus, "telling us we couldn't have Indians that were given to us by the King, the lord of all these Indies, especially after we Spaniards won all these islands with much effort and brought these unbelievers into subjection. You need to retract what you said, Father."

Montesinos and Córdoba listened quietly.

"If not," the Governor added ominously, "we will remedy things ourselves."

Córdoba calmly informed the delegation that Montesinos had represented the sentiments of all the Dominicans quite clearly and with their approval.

"We were sent to these islands by His Majesty to preach the Gospel and the truth," Córdoba told them. "Spaniards and Indians are both perishing daily, you Spaniards for treating the Indians as if they were nothing more than animals, and the Indians for lack of hearing the Word and accepting the Faith." That the Indians may have not wanted either the Spaniards OR their religion probably escaped the world view of these sixteenth-century Catholic religious warriors who believed passionately in their right and obligation to evangelize all. It was a form of Christian imperialism common to the era and consistent with the temper of the times.

Córdoba continued, "We are sure if His Majesty [Ferdinand; Queen Isabella had passed away] were well informed on what was happening here, and what we preachers did, he would be giving us thanks for having served him so well."

The gauntlet had been thrown down at the feet of the new lords of the land by these few mendicant friars. At issue was none other than the power of the Church versus the power of the State. Faced with such an intrepid spirit, the governor and others backed down a bit.

"You *have* [emphasis added] to moderate what you said in that sermon, Father. The settlers are scandalized by your accusations."

To mollify them, Córdoba promised them that Father Montesinos would preach again next Sunday, and that he would touch on the same subjects, and he would say what he feels is best, and clarify what he can.

Satisfied, "they left happy with this hope," recorded Las Casas, expecting a retraction next Sunday.

What a surprise was in store! Expecting a public retraction, the settlers packed the small church to see this priest humble himself before the notables of the island. Montesinos—in close collaboration with his fellow friars—chose as his Scripture, Job 36: 3–4.

> I get my knowledge from afar;
> I will ascribe justice to my Maker.

Be assured that my words are not false;
one perfect in knowledge is with you.

Once the Scripture was read, Montesinos closed the Bible and looked up to face the congregation. In fact, most of the city's Spanish citizens were packed in.

"Let me turn to what we covered last Sunday," Montesinos began. "Those words you found so bitter to take, they were in fact the truth."[17]

Everyone knew where the priest was going after that opening. Montesinos was not meekly retracting and conforming to their wishes. Not only did Montesinos ratify his message of the previous week, but he also told his hearers that they would not be offered the Sacraments unless they repented and ceased their evil against the Indians. Montesinos added that they could complain to Spain if they desired.

"We are serving God for sure, and it's no small service to the King as well." With that parting shot, Montesinos stepped down from the pulpit, and took his place in history at one of its most crucial junctures. The battle had been joined.

Las Casas, however, had other things on his mind. While he faithfully later recorded for his *History* this first confrontation between the Dominicans and the settlers, he was preparing to leave the island on a journey that set the stage for the rest of his life's work. Late in 1511, Diego de Velázquez was sent by Diego Columbus to conquer Cuba, and Las Casas was invited by Velázquez to join him on this expedition.

Las Casas goes to Cuba

The Spanish campaign in Cuba began with a hunt for the Taino chieftain Hatuey. He had fled from the Spanish in Española across the Windward Passage to Cuba, only to find himself pursued by dogs and horses led by Velázquez and his military commander, Pánfilo de Narváez. The mounted, mobile Spaniards seemed to be everywhere and there was no escape. What happened was recorded by Las Casas. Once captured, the Spaniards determined to burn Hatuey at the stake, "guilty of *lèse majesté*."[18] What was Hatuey guilty of? Las Casas answered rhetorically:

Nothing more than "flee his home island to keep from being killed and persecuted in such a horrible, cruel, and tyrannical manner."

Having tied him to the stake, Las Casas recorded, a Franciscan begged Hatuey to be baptized and die a Christian.

"Why would I want to be like the Christians, who are evil?" shot back Hatuey.

"Because those who die as Christians go to heaven and are in the presence of God enjoying themselves forever."

Hatuey turned to the priest. "Do Christians go to heaven?"

"All those who are good," responded the friar.

"Well, I don't want to go where Spaniards go."

The executioners then applied the torch to the faggots and burned the man alive. Las Casas reflected bitterly on these events.

"This was the justice meted out to those who fled from evil and cruelty … This was the honor given to God who blessed us with his redeeming blood … What else could he [Hatuey] say except that he didn't want to go to heaven because that's where Christians were? How could it be a 'good place' where such bad men lived for eternity?"

How right Hatuey had been, Las Casas reflected, when he warned his people that there was one God above all the Spanish worshipped: the god of gold.

Soon after the execution of Hatuey, told to him by eye witnesses, Las Casas arrived in Cuba and joined the company of Pánfilo de Narváez. From then until early in 1515, Las Casas followed loosely in the company of Narváez in the conquest and pacification of Cuba.

Velázquez founded the town of Baracoa on the northeastern tip of Cuba and dispatched Narváez westwards into the island towards a region called the Bayamo. For the next three years Las Casas served in an increasingly ambiguous situation. Las Casas the priest promoted the peaceful pacification of the peoples of Cuba, baptizing children, teaching adults, converting by persuasion and kindness. On the other hand, he continued to acquire Indians in *encomienda*—bestowed upon him by his friend and patron Governor Velázquez—Indians who worked in the fields and gold mines for Las Casas and added to his growing wealth. Eventually the strain of living two lives pushed him to the most important decision in his life. One event, more than any other, drove Las Casas across his own Rubicon.

Nearing the town of Caonao in the eastern third of the island, the Spaniards, following a dry riverbed, came upon some large boulders. They unsheathed and whetted their swords, maybe joking about their sharpness and bragging a bit as soldiers are wont to do. They arrived near sunset at Caonao where two thousand Indians were gathered peacefully. The Indians watched the Spaniards and their horses, still flabbergasted by these huge animals, as Narváez's warriors filed into the town, swords sharpened, senses alert. Five hundred more Indians huddled in a large *bohío*, or house, terrified by the sight and sounds of the thundering horses and Spanish knights. Outside the house, the Spanish received gifts of cassava bread and fish prepared by the Indians.

Suddenly, a Spaniard unsheathed his sword and others followed suit. "They fell upon those sheep and lambs, slashing, disemboweling, and killing them."[19] Women and men, children and elders, none were spared. "In the span it takes to say two *credos*, they were all killed." The Spaniards stormed into the *bohío* and slaughtered the Indians cowering in that place. Blood ran like a slaughterhouse for cattle.

Las Casas thought the devil got into them. He speculated in a more secular vein that some Spaniards thought the Indians, adorned with sharp fish bones as was their custom, intended to ambush them. Or, the small ropes they carried around their waists were to bind the mounted warriors once they were captured. None of this made any sense to him.

Amidst the killing Narváez saw Las Casas. "Well, your mercy, what do you think of the boys, of what they've done?" Narváez remarked nonchalantly.

Las Casas stood stunned, looking around, finally blurting out, "Both you and your boys go to hell!"

Narváez, on horseback, sat like a statue, silent, unmoving, and watched as the slaughter unfolded. Mounted, armored, lance in hand, he could have stepped in and stopped it. Desperate, Las Casas rushed after the Spaniards in the surrounding woods still pursuing the fleeing Indians. "Stop, stop, you mad fools! Stop! Have mercy!"

Only the darkness of the night slowed down the massacre. But the nightmare was not yet over. Returning to the *bohío* where five hundred had been slaughtered, Las Casas found a few souls still alive, clinging to the rafters where they had escaped the slashing Spaniards.

"Come down, come down," Las Casas urged them. "You're safe. It's ended. Don't be afraid. It's ended. Come down." Hearing the priest, one young man descended slowly, crying as he lowered himself. Las Casas left the *bohío* to intercede in other places between the Spaniards and the surviving Indians. A Spaniard in the *bohío* saw the Indian. The soldier drew his short sword and, with a quick thrust and slash, opened the Indian's guts which spilled out. The Indian grabbed his innards and staggered outside where he ran into Las Casas.

"Oh, my God. You can't live long, son," Las Casas said in anguish. "Accept baptism so you go and live with God forever."

"Yes, Father, yes," the Indian responded, dropping and dying at the priest's feet in the act of being baptized.

Las Casas did his best over the next week to help the survivors, sewing up wounds, cauterizing others, applying ointments, such as the fat of turtles, to speed up the healing process. Those who survived fled to the small islands off the south coast of Cuba, those Columbus had named the "Garden of the Queen." The contrast between the arrogant and merciless Narváez and the compassionate priest Las Casas struck the Indians of Cuba as strange and inconsistent. It was also apparent that these invaders—some monstrous and some kind—would not be going away.

Las Casas turned a corner after the Caonao massacre. The gulf between Christian doctrine and acts such as this senseless massacre was growing wider, more and more difficult to reconcile. In the meantime, Governor Velázquez continued to favor Las Casas and honor him with gifts of Indians as the world struggled with his spirit for control of his heart and mind.

The devastation of Cuba was well underway, as Spaniards crisscrossed the island in search of Indians to "pacify" and put to work in the mines. Without giving the Indians respite to plant and work their fields, human resources were soon depleted and hunger set in rapidly. The strong were taken off to work in the fields and mines, leaving only the sick and the old in the villages with no one to care and feed them. They died in waves of anguish and starvation.[20]

Unlike the Tainos of Española, however, not all the Arawaks of Cuba perished in this inferno set off by the Spanish approach.[21] Many fled the

Spaniards to the small islands off the north coast of Cuba, to the Florida Keys, to the islands of the Bahamas and even to the Florida peninsula.[22] Of the Arawak population of about 150,000–200,000 on the island, the Spanish only successfully "reduced" maybe 20,000 or 30,000 into *encomiendas*. Probably half these died in later waves of smallpox.[23] Las Casas's testimony, no matter how moving and horrifying, must be assessed critically in the light of modern research which sometimes confirms his figures of Amerindians at the time of contact—the numbers often considered wildly exaggerated by his critics—while just as often correcting them in the light of new techniques of studying demographics. Nonetheless, even though substantial numbers of Arawaks survived the conquest and live to this day in Cuba, Las Casas's account is heartrendingly true in the main.

Las Casas himself admitted to an earlier callousness in the face of so much suffering and misery. He too had sent his Indians to the gold mines or into the fields, forgetting the obligation to teach them Christian doctrine and bring them into the brotherhood of the Church. That none of this made any sense to the Amerindians is perhaps transparently self-evident. Their world was being destroyed by invaders who demanded everything from them, stripping them not only of their lives and property but also of their spirit world and gods.

Then Providence intervened in Las Casas's life. Governor Velázquez asked him to celebrate Mass and preach to the Spaniards at the newly-founded city of Sant Espíritus in south central Cuba, not far from Las Casas's own *encomienda* at Canarreo near modern Cienfuegos. The feast of Pentecost, 1514, was fast approaching. Las Casas searched Scripture for an appropriate passage that reflected his troubled state of mind, one that gave light to what so shadowed his heart.

"And, if I haven't forgotten," Las Casas remembered, "something from Ecclesiasticus 34 came to mind."[24] The words and their message sank deeply into his heart as he considered their meaning in the light of his experiences in the New World.

"If one sacrifices from what has been wrongfully obtained, the offering is blemished; the gifts of the lawless are not acceptable."

"The Most High is not pleased with the offerings of the ungodly; and he is not propitiated for sins by a multitude of sacrifices."

"Like one who kills a son before his father's eyes is the man who offers a sacrifice from the property of the poor."

"The bread of the needy is the life of the poor; whoever deprives them of it is a man of blood."[25]

Las Casas reflected on the misery and servitude that those peoples had been plunged into, much of which he witnessed. He remembered what the Dominicans on Española had said and done. They refused to confess Spaniards—including himself—who continued to hold Indians in *encomienda*.

"He spent some days thinking about the situation, each day getting surer and surer from what he read concerning what was legal and what was actual, measuring the one by the other, until he came to the same truth [as the Dominicans] by himself."

Las Casas pored through other Scriptures as well as Ecclesiasticus. Indeed, "everything he read affirmed his decision."[26] Bolstered by Scripture, conditioned by his association with the Dominicans, and burned by experience, Las Casas freed his *encomienda* Indians and prepared his sermon. He took to the pulpit and reminded his listeners of the spiritual and corporal works of mercy according to the Scripture reading for the day.

"These works must also be performed on behalf of those people," Las Casas began, "who have been so cruelly treated. You must cease to live off of them with such neglect, so mindlessly, so failing in your obligations." After chastising his listeners a bit more, he broke the news that he himself had given away all his Indians and had ended his life as an *encomendero*. Astonished, they listened now with total concentration to the priest, until now one of them. Las Casas laid bare their sins. He pilloried their blindness, their injustices, their tyrannies, and their cruelties inflicted on such an innocent and gentle people. And, as he revealed the awful consequence of sin, his voice and message resonated with the same thunder of the ancient prophets of Israel.

"You cannot be saved while still holding Indians!" Only by making full restitution, by giving up their *encomienda*s as he had, could they hope to avoid the fiery lake of eternal fire. He condemned both those who held the Indians and those who distributed them, added to ensure that no one, including Governor Velázquez, felt above the scourge of truth, the anticipation of God's judgment on their eternal lives. Justice, before God and man, if it was to be true justice, had to be for all humankind.

Las Casas then reflected on the effect of his words. And before him he had his answer. "They were all astonished, some even grieved and saddened by what he said. Others thought it was a bad dream, hearing the strange news that they could not hold Indians in service without sinning, as if telling them that they couldn't use beasts of the field. It was unbelievable!"

The priest and prophet left the congregation buzzing with a mixture of fear and indignation. But he soon realized he could do little to change the carnage in the Indies by himself. He decided to go straight to the top, in this case to King Ferdinand. In late 1515, he crossed the Atlantic on this mission, his spirit lighted by his newly discovered empowerment and determination to do God's will and save the Indians of the New World. If only the King knew the truth. Now he would. First, however, on his way to Spain he traveled to Santo Domingo to speak with his spiritual mentor, Father Pedro de Córdoba, the vicar of the Dominicans.

Córdoba assigned Father Antonio de Montesinos to accompany Las Casas on his return to Spain. Moreover, the tiny Dominican community in Santo Domingo was poverty-stricken, suffering great want, and Córdoba instructed Montesinos to beg the King for some alms to build a proper church and home for the friars.

Under the provisions of an agreement called the Royal Patronage negotiated between Ferdinand and the Papacy a few years earlier, the Crown of Spain obtained a significant degree of control over the Church in the Indies. In return for allowing the monarchs of Spain a good deal of authority in the naming and appointment of clergy to the Indies, in establishing bishoprics, and in other ways controlling the Church, the Crown agreed to support the Church's endeavors—such as the missionary work of the Franciscans and Dominicans—with not only royal authority but also financial support. The Church and State in the newly developing Spanish Empire in the Americas thus came to be closely bonded by the common interests of establishing both royal and ecclesiastical authority in the Indies. Asking the King for alms was but a formula for claiming what the Crown had promised to the Church within the larger context of the Royal Patronage.

Figure 2.3   Father Pedro de Córdoba, the saintly, self-sacrificing Dominican who first traveled to Española in 1510 and there, with other Dominicans, first preached against the Conquest, deeply influencing the course of Las Casas's life, and the search for justice among a small but influential group of Spaniards.

To Spain

Early in September, 1515, Las Casas embarked for Spain. It was a quick passage, a good voyage, in his own words. Las Casas crossed the Atlantic at least eight times in his lifetime. His world was not bounded by Spain, by Española, by Cuba, or by any other of the Indies that he eventually traveled through in his lifetime—Venezuela, Panama, Nicaragua, Guatemala, Mexico, for example. He became one of the individuals whose earliest Atlantic travels pioneered a new world, one broadly labeled the "Atlantic world." Bounded by Europe, Africa, and the Americas, the Atlantic world encompassed all three, and much of the dynamics of our modern Western world were fashioned in this vast space of land and water interconnected by travelers, trade, culture, migration, and war.[27] Europe was breaking out from the geographic parochialism that had marked the Middle Ages and it exploded into the world with high energy, driven by visionary men such as Columbus and Las Casas. After a quick crossing, Las Casas arrived in his hometown of Seville on October 6.

The Spain which Las Casas returned to for the first time since he left in 1502 was buzzing with news of voyages of exploration and new discoveries in the lands and islands on the other side of the great Ocean Sea (Atlantic). Las Casas fit perfectly into this rapidly evolving and dynamic new society which, in his mind, however, was seriously flawed in the Indies by injustice. To right the injustice, Las Casas was headed to see the King.

Las Casas felt he had a right to expect justice from King Ferdinand since, in the theory and practice of monarchy, the King was the ultimate adjudicator in the land, the final judge. The Old Testament, a well from which Las Casas often drew deeply, was quite clear that Kings were anointed by God, and "Kings detest wrongdoing ... Kings take pleasure in honest lips ... they value a man who speaks the truth" [Proverbs 16:13].

Las Casas's growing erudition and reading gave him a broad intellectual and spiritual platform. Very much a child of the humanistic Renaissance like many of his generation, he probed deeply into Scripture, and drew much of the justification for his mission from the Bible. The reformist, humanist spirit of the Renaissance challenged the often decadent and corrupt ways of many churchmen of the times. The reformers turned to the early principles of Christianity as expressed in Scripture itself, to the Early Church Fathers, and especially were influenced by some of Christianity's most profound thinkers, principally among them St. Augustine of Hippo and St. Thomas Aquinas.

Once back in Seville in October, 1515, Montesinos presented Las Casas to the Archbishop of Seville, the Dominican friar, Diego de Deza.

"He is like one of us, Your Excellency," Montesinos told the Archbishop.

Kneeling and kissing the hands of the Archbishop, Las Casas listened as Montesinos described Las Casas's efforts in defense of the Indians.[28]

"You are doing well, doing well, Father," Archbishop Deza told Las Casas. Deza provided Las Casas with letters of introduction, one to the King and another to members of his retinue. With those letters, Las Casas caught up with Ferdinand in December, 1515. In the meantime, he learned of the corrupting effect the *encomienda* of the Indies was having in Spain itself.

Gold from Española and Cuba was swelling the ranks of the newly rich, and increasing the stake of royal officials, high-ranked churchmen, and other well-placed bureaucrats in Castile who held *encomienda* Indians *in absentia*. The King himself was the largest holder of Indians and thus had a growing stake in the system of forced labor as it evolved. Two of his closest counselors, Secretary Lope Conchillos and Juan Rodríguez de Fonseca, the Bishop of Burgos in charge of the Indies, were profiting from their *encomienda* Indians. Las Casas faced a difficult uphill battle, but adversity only hardened his resolve.

Meeting Ferdinand

Las Casas finally met Ferdinand during the Christmas season of 1515, in the city of Plasencia, in the province of Extremadura, hundreds of miles north of Seville. It was cold. Extremadura in wintertime is a gloomy, forbidding part of the Castilian high plains. The King was sick, uncomfortable, and perhaps well aware that he was dying. Worldly matters, matters of State, matters of truth and justice, were probably far from his mind when Las Casas, one priest among thousands in Spain, secured an audience. Suspecting Secretary Conchillos and Bishop Fonseca, both holding large *encomienda* grants, might sabotage any meeting, Las Casas somehow arranged to meet privately with Ferdinand.

"One night," Las Casas remembered, "on the eve of the Eve of the Birth of our Redeemer, I talked with the King for a long time."[29]

"Your Majesty," the olive-complexioned Sevillan with piercing eyes started right in. "What is happening in your possessions is nothing less than a disaster, both in God's eyes and, now I'm here to tell you, in yours as well." Las Casas proceeded rapidly.[30]

"The islands' people are being destroyed, dying violent deaths, going to perdition without benefit of the Church. Greed is remorselessly destroying them and if Your Majesty doesn't come to their rescue soon, there will be nothing left but a desert on these islands, once paradises, now infernos."

Wracked by pains eating away at his lower body, Ferdinand, almost semi-conscious, nonetheless listened. There was something about this priest, an intensity, a focus, and a message that one could not easily turn aside.

"Not only is God offended, Your Majesty, by the cupidity and brutality of the *encomenderos*, but your rents will soon peter out with no one to work the fields, to labor in the mines."

Was this priest right? Were such abominations really being done in his name? Earlier, in 1512, Ferdinand had listened to another priest describe the cruelties on the islands. He signed the Laws of Burgos—the first royal efforts to reduce the abuses of the Indians through legislation—but they were obeyed largely in the breach.[31] Now this new priest accosted him with renewed vigor. But Ferdinand was tired. Even the self-confident, sometimes egotistical Las Casas sensed the audience was over.

Las Casas then asked for a longer audience when the court reached Seville. Ferdinand agreed and ended this meeting that so troubled his spirit. He turned over Las Casas's letter of introduction from the Archbishop of Seville to Secretary Conchillos. The next day Las Casas met with the King's confessor, Tomás Matienzo. He sympathized with Las Casas, who was nonetheless disappointed by the audience with Ferdinand. It was obvious that the King was drifting away to death and his thoughts were turning in on himself, his pain, his forthcoming passage.

Matienzo counseled Las Casas to be patient, wait until Seville, they could have a full hearing then.

"You haven't spoken with Secretary Conchillos or Bishop Fonseca yet," chided Matienzo.

"Why?" asked Las Casas. "They hold Indians in *encomienda*, they're getting rich off the oppression of these peoples. How can I expect anything of them?"

True, Matienzos probably thought, but, still, this priest has much to learn. "But you can't leave them without an interview. It is only politic. It would make your case worse to ignore them." So Las Casas requested an audience with both these powerful men.

Conchillos was smooth and superficially warm and friendly. He flattered Las Casas and offered him perquisites or honors based on his long and dutiful experience in the Indies. Put all this business behind you, Conchillos suggested fraternally.

"We have need of visionary and forthright people like you, Father, right here in Castile." But Las Casas resisted the blandishments, the honey-covered words, the subtle attempts to buy him off.

"I was little moved by the soft and attractive offers of the Secretary," Las Casas recorded a few years later, "by the hopes that I would leave the mission which God himself had inspired in me." Las Casas had put aside his love of money. He credited God with miraculously taking away greed for temporal things.

Las Casas next met with Bishop Fonseca. If the wily and silver-tongued Conchillos was the serpent, tempting with guile and promises, Fonseca minced no words. He represented the unvarnished reality of the world and Las Casas was shocked by the interview. They met one night, still in Plasencia, still in the Christmas season. Las Casas came armed with his petition, describing the horrors and atrocities in the islands. It was a long petition, and it became Las Casas's hallmark, his calling card.

Talking at length, Las Casas finished his presentation with his *coup de grâce*, the murder of 7000 children in three short months in Cuba. The 75-year-old Fonseca, filled with pride and ill-humored at best, was quickly bored by the tiresome priest. He had listened long enough.

"Look, this is simply stupid. What do I care? And what does the King care?"[32]

The fire ignited in Las Casas. "It doesn't mean anything," he shouted back at the Bishop of Burgos, the administrator of the King's Indies, "that all those souls were killed?! Great God almighty! Then who should care!" Las Casas turned and stormed out of the chamber and the Bishop's residence. The Bishop's clients and petitioners, some of them recently returned from the Indies, erupted in laughter at the sight of the priest's loud exit. Frustrated by Conchillos and maddened by Fonseca, Las Casas returned to his native Seville to await the King's arrival. Ferdinand, however, died on January 25, 1516, before ever reaching Seville.

Now what? The King is dead, long live the King. The crown eventually passed to Ferdinand's grandson, the young Prince Charles, then in Flanders. Las Casas quickly determined his next step. On to Flanders.

Dynastic politics in Europe was not that simple, Las Casas soon discovered. To begin with, Charles was not a Spaniard. Born in the city of Ghent in Flanders in 1500, he was raised far away from Castile and did not even speak Spanish. His grandparents included not only Queen Isabel and King Ferdinand, but also Emperor Maximilian I of Austria and Germany and Maximilian's wife, Mary of Burgundy. This pedigree eventually secured him the throne of Spain (1516) and election as Holy Roman Emperor (1519). His kingdoms as a Habsburg included the Netherlands, Austria, the Kingdom of Naples, and much of Germany. By birthright principally, and astute political maneuvering, he ascended to a position of dominance among the monarchs of sixteenth-century Europe, this all before the age of 21. In Spain, he was Charles I; as Holy Roman Emperor, he was Charles V.

Adrian of Utrecht, who later became Pope Adrian VI in 1522, advised Charles spiritually as he grew up in the Netherlands. Adrian, the only Dutch pope and the last non-Italian elected to the Papacy until 1978 (John Paul II, a Pole), was a reformer, intellectual and never too far from Charles's side. Upon Ferdinand's death in early 1516, Adrian was appointed co-regent of Spain along with Cardinal Francisco Ximénez de Cisneros. Adrian joined Cisneros in Madrid to help him govern Spain and await the arrival of Charles. Both regents were prelates, both were reformers, both represented the power of the monarchy.

Las Casas found both regents, Adrian and Cisneros, lodging in close proximity in Madrid. This was indeed providential he must have thought. He first approached Adrian, and then Cisneros.

Las Casas prepared a long memorial to present his arguments. Since Adrian did not read Spanish, Las Casas wrote one version in Latin for him. Adrian was shocked by the revelations of cruelty which Las Casas described in vivid detail. He then went over to Cardinal Cisneros' quarters and presented him with the same document in Spanish, although the learned Franciscan could of course read Latin, the language of the Church.

The old Spanish cardinal was better informed than Adrian on the matter of Spanish behavior, or misbehavior in the Indies. His Franciscan brethren kept him apprised and so Las Casas did not shock or surprise Cisneros. After all, the reformist Laws of Burgos, drawn up in 1512, themselves testified to the situation in the Indies.

"Father," Cisneros told Las Casas. "There's no need for you to go further, to Flanders [to petition Charles]. We'll take care of this matter here."[33]

Cisneros was as good as his word. He asked Las Casas to return and present his accusations to a larger forum, which included Adrian and several other Spanish jurists. In the meantime, Cardinal Cisneros had sacked Bishop Fonseca from his post as overseer of the Indies in April, and he wanted to get rid of the powerful Secretary Conchillos as well. Las Casas kept up a drumbeat of accusations in the air all spring and early summer of 1516, and Cisneros listened, even as he was occupied with many other matters of state.[34] In June, a commission was convened by Cisneros to review the application and effectiveness of the Laws of Burgos. This commission included Las Casas who was asked to compose the first draft of their report.[35]

One day the commission convened with both Regents—Cisneros and Adrian—in attendance. Cisneros wanted particularly to ascertain what the Laws of Burgos said on the *encomienda*.[36] Proponents of the *encomienda* said the Laws specifically allowed for the institution, while Las Casas was pushing for its complete elimination. In this, he was supported by Adrian.

"Besides, Your Mercies," Las Casas addressed Cisneros and Adrian, "the Laws of Burgos were subverted by the *encomenderos* who ignored them altogether and went about their business without the least conscience."

"Well," responded one of Secretary Conchillos' representatives at this meeting, "that may be, but certainly the King and members of the Council were deceived into believing the Laws were being applied."

"Hah!" snorted Las Casas. "They were deceived because they were disingenuous. They too were getting rich off the *encomienda*."[37] Las Casas knew he was stepping on the memory of the dead King Ferdinand, but he was, after all, dead.

Cardinal Cisneros warmly endorsed the ongoing work of the commission. With Las Casas taking the lead in drafting, they soon produced a document, *A Remedy for the Indies*. It is one of the most extraordinary documents in the history of colonization, a plan to save the Indians within the context of the ongoing Spanish exploration and settlement of the Americas.

Las Casas's philosophical doctrines in the *Remedy* transcend time and place. Las Casas insisted on the basic liberty of all people and, equally important, on their *right* to life.

"Of interest here," wrote Gustavo Gutiérrez, one of Las Casas's most discerning modern biographers, "is that, for Las Casas, life is [not only] the natural right of every human being, but it also is a gift of God, and so a believer ought to respect and defend it."[38]

Indians are "free human beings," Las Casas wrote, "and ought to be treated as human beings and free." Freedom is absolutely essential if the Gospel is to be received by peaceful evangelization. This was the only way to spread the Word in Las Casas's mind.

He furthermore insisted that the only reason for the Spaniards to be in the Indies was to evangelize. To do this properly, and in accordance with the Gospel of Jesus Christ, it had to be done peacefully, without violence to the hearers. And the hearers must be free to accept or reject the Word of salvation and redemption.

Drawing up the *Remedy* engrossed Las Casas that spring and summer of 1516. He was making history, a heady and intoxicating activity. He composed feverishly, drawing on his prodigious memory of what he had witnessed, and propelled by a powerful and creative imagination as to what should be. The *Remedy* contained 14 points, the principal one being freeing the Indians from under *encomendero* control.

No remedy will work, Las Casas insisted, if the Indians remain in the power of the Spaniards. So, point one was to radically reform the *encomienda*s which were, in Las Casas's mind, the instrument of oppression. The rest of the *Remedy* consisted of an incredibly detailed plan "that is most startling … every detail of the Indians' lives is regulated … every possible contingency is provided for."[39]

There were parts of the *Remedy* that still cause controversy today. In the eleventh remedy, dealing with the mines, Las Casas suggested that "twenty blacks, or other slaves" be employed. This unremarkable throwaway line has blacklisted Las Casas as one of the founders and promoters of African slavery in the New World, a hypocrite to the bone who defended the Indians but cast blacks into the perdition of plantation slavery of the Americas.[40] In 1516, however, his entire focus was basically on the Indians and drafting the *Remedy*.

When presented with the *Remedy*, Cardinal Cisneros asked the Order of St. Jerome, the Hieronymites, to take on the task of implementing these reforms. Translating the victory at court in Castile to action in the Indies was another matter, as Las Casas soon discovered, and rediscovered over the years.

3

Social Experiments
The Hieronymite Mission and the Universal Protector of All the Indians

Once the order of the Hieronymites had been selected, Las Casas prepared for the return to the Indies. While the Hieronymites were not the most committed of reformers, they were certainly many cuts above the greedy settlers and their advocates at court.[1] Las Casas also had received an extraordinary commission from the Cardinal, one that has been associated with him for the last five hundred years. Las Casas was named "universal protector of all the Indians of the Indies," and he has come down to us through the years as the "protector of the Indians," sometimes translated as the "defender of Indians."[2]

In addition to his new title, Las Casas was ordered by Cisneros and Adrian to accompany the Hieronymite mission and assist them in reforming the Indies on all matters touching upon the "liberty and good treatment and health of the souls and bodies of the Indians." Las Casas and the Hieronymite friars set sail on November 11, 1516, and made a quick crossing, arriving in Santo Domingo about mid-December.

For the next six months, or to about June or July, 1517, Las Casas waged his war against the settlers, the *encomienda*, and the lucrative Indian slave trading business, while the Hieronymites made lukewarm attempts at reform. To the Hieronymites, the matter was clear. Initiating drastic reforms meant rebellion. So, like all bureaucrats over the ages, they waffled.

Bartolomé de las Casas and the Conquest of the Americas. Lawrence A. Clayton
© 2011 Lawrence A. Clayton

Las Casas was constantly in the commissioners' faces. "I visited them often. I explained the way to free and thus conserve the lives of the Indians. I brought them witnesses to the brutality meted out to the Indians. The fathers heard me, but they didn't do anything."[3]

Las Casas, on the other hand, was not plagued by doubt. His demands to free the Indians from the control of royal officials was so strident, and the murmuring against him at such a level, that his Dominican friends feared for his safety. They persuaded him to spend his nights in their quarters, and he did so for the next four or five months, venturing only out in safety during the daylight hours.

Nothing could mollify Las Casas. When the Hieronymites began their official judicial investigation, they asked leading questions that allowed the settlers to explain away their behavior in ways all too familiar to Las Casas and the Dominicans: the Indians are barbarians; they are incapable of governing themselves; if not instructed by the Spaniards, they will waste away and die; they are primitive, unpolitical animals. Las Casas charged the already electric atmosphere even more with powerful denunciations of royal officials. "They are murderers and deserve to die," the fiery priest accused the *encomenderos* and royal officials who still held Indians either in servitude or slavery.[4]

Whatever latent sympathy Las Casas may have had with the Hieronymites was gone by spring of 1517. They sent a long letter on May 4 to Cardinal Cisneros accusing Las Casas of undermining their authority, of distorting the truth, of raising rebellion. Las Casas answered with his own letters. He claimed his were intercepted while those of the Hieronymites made it through to Spain.

The *encomenderos*, fearing the loss of their livelihood if this fanatical priest and his Dominican friends had their way, worked the Indians even more brutally, hoping to get as much gold out of the earth before the Indians were taken away from them. Women, children, even pregnant women, were all exploited with even greater vigor. Ironically, the plan to lift the oppressive mantle of the Spanish regime off the Indians was redoubling their pain. Las Casas decided to return to Spain. He could do no more here on the islands.

He left in May, arriving back in Seville some time in July. He soon left for Aranda de Duero, in the north of Castile where he found Cardinal Cisneros close to death. Las Casas secured an audience, but the Cardinal hardly recognized the younger priest and died within a few days. For Las Casas, the failure of the Hieronymites' reforms only added propellant to his mission. The Cardinal was dead. But King Charles I was coming to town.

Undeterred by the failures of the Hieronymites, Las Casas determined that the next reform of the Indies would be in his hands. For the next four years, 1518–1522, he turned his focus to Tierra Firme, a name the Spanish used rather loosely for the northern mainland of South America, principally the Atlantic/Caribbean coastlines of modern Venezuela, Colombia, and Panama. The many Indian peoples along those coasts were already feeling the effects of slave raids, armed expeditions, and diseases, but it was an immense continent. It could still be saved.

Before he could save Tierra Firme, however, Las Casas needed permission to do so. Not one to wait on the hand of God, Las Casas jumped into the middle of young King Charles's Flemish entourage and gained the ascendancy over his Spanish rivals at court. Las Casas's next three years at court were a masterpiece of lobbying, maneuvering, and persuasion. He used, primarily, the natural suspicion of Charles' Flemish advisers for old King Ferdinand's Castilian nobles who were, in the main, Las Casas's rivals. That Cardinal Adrian remembered Las Casas well was another trump card for Las Casas. Adrian was close to Charles, having served as tutor for the young prince since 1506.

Las Casas traveled to Valladolid, a university city and one of the old capitals of Castile, where he met up with Reginaldo de Montesinos, the brother of Antonio de Montesinos who had preached the sermon in Santo Domingo in 1511. Reginaldo Montesinos and Las Casas knew each other from their student days at the school of Santo Tomás in Seville where Las Casas had learned to read and write Latin. Reginaldo too was awaiting the Court's arrival in Castile.

Montesinos wished to petition Charles on behalf of the Dominicans of Andalucia to give them support to protect their brothers on the Pearl Coast of Tierra Firme (eastern Venezuela) where they had a small mission at Chiribichi. The Franciscans also had a mission nearby, slightly to the east at Cumaná. Offshore was the island of Cubagua where some of the richest pearl fisheries in the world had been discovered a few years earlier by Spanish explorers and adventurers. All of this was making for a dynamic brew. The friars denounced the pearl hunters and slavers; the latter disdained these self-righteous priests who constantly took the side of the barbarians and cannibals. The friars were barely hanging on, threatened by the very Indians they were trying to convert. In the Indians' minds all Spaniards came out of the same nest of vipers.

The Amerindian view of the approach of the Spaniards has engaged scholars over the past half century as never before. The traditional history of the Encounter has been, necessarily so, Eurocentric, or told from within the European perspective, or point of view. Most written records of the Spanish armed expeditions into the Americas were kept, obviously, by the conquistador-settler class, or, equally important, by their competitors for the hearts and souls of the Amerindians, the priests and friars like Las Casas. However, Amerindians were not all illiterate.

As usual, the truth is more complicated than a simple generality can encompass. The Maya did have a form of writing—hieroglyphs—which are a fairly sophisticated form of written language in which most of the symbols represent syllables such as ka, la, ba, and so forth. It's a syllabary, and like Egyptian hieroglyphs, you can write anything you can say. Mayan scribes were still reading and writing paper books (codices) into the sixteenth century. In his passion to destroy Maya idolatry, Franciscan Bishop Diego de Landa tried to burn every Maya book he could get his hands on in 1562, but ironically he did preserve the basic "alphabet" in his long report on his experiences in Yucatán, *Relación de las cosas de Yucatán*.[5] On the other hand, neither the Aztec nor the Inca had a phonetic written language, although Inca record keeping, through a system of *quipus*, or colored threads with knots, was quite sophisticated.

Later, when Spanish friars created grammars of Amerindian languages, a few records of the conquest were composed by Amerindians themselves. These constitute an important source for the Amerindian perspective. Nonetheless, the major sources for the Amerindian reaction to the European invasion were produced by the priests and friars themselves. And, of these, none rose to the stature, or was so strident for so long, in defense of Indian rights as Las Casas.

Not only did he attack his fellow Spaniards, but he also took the side of the Amerindians, speaking for them and defending their right to resist the advance of Spanish warriors, even under the thinly disguised excuse of bringing them to Christianity, and thus saving their eternal souls. There was in fact kind of a civil war going on between Spaniards—the conquistadors and those we label the anti-conquistadors—even while the Spanish conquistadors themselves warred on the Amerindians.

The entire epoch is seen in retrospect by one scholar as a polemic or argument between Spaniards and representatives of Amerindian culture over the rights of Spanish dominion in the Americas and the treatment of its natives.[6] Central to this argument is Las Casas, the spokesman, in his own mind, of the Amerindian.

Yet, at the time, it was difficult for the people of the Caribbean islands and along the coasts of Tierra Firme being slaughtered and exploited by the Spaniards to distinguish between these two sides of the Spanish character. So the urgency of the moment drove Las Casas and Reginaldo Montesinos to hurry their business with the King, for the liberty, the rights, and the very lives of the Indians were at stake.

Montesinos was trained as a cleric and a scholar, and he, like Las Casas, pursued the defense of the Indians with vigor. To gather allies for his cause, he wrote his friend Juan Hurtado, the Dominican prior of the monastery of Santisteban [San Esteban or St. Stephen's] at Salamanca. Hurtado was widely known in the Dominican Order as an exemplary scholar. He was a member of the faculty at the famed University of Salamanca founded in 1215, a center of humanistic learning in Europe. Hurtado in turn convened a pioneering meeting of thirteen of the University's scholars to consider the question: Are the Indians capable of accepting and understanding the Faith? This was probably the first time this question on the nature of the native people of the Americas was framed in such a fashion and as such is a major building block in the history of human rights.[7]

These theologian/scholars issued four or five conclusions, with evidence and proofs. Among them was the unsurprising one that, yes, Father Montesinos was right, and his critics completely in error. Then they added a startling judgment: And, if the anti-Indianists persisted in defending their errors, they were heretics and merited the death penalty.

"All of the proceedings from this committee came signed," Las Casas wrote, "and authorized by the signatories. I saw them and translated them [perhaps from Latin to Castilian]. In fact, I would include them in this account [Las Casas's *History of the Indies*] verbatim, except that, along with other documents, somebody stole them along some road, and so they were lost to me."[8]

These were powerful declarations. Later Las Casas and other Spanish jurists and theologians raised the stakes even higher, from a consideration of the nature of the Amerindians to questioning the very legitimacy of the Spanish claims to sovereignty in the New World. Spain claimed her position in the Indies by virtue of the rights of discovery, the Papal Donation of 1493, and the Treaty of Tordesillas of 1494 between Spain and Portugal. The scholars of Salamanca concluded otherwise: the *only* reason for Spain to be in the New World was to evangelize. Any other reasons were spurious; they contradicted the basic rights of people to be free. The Salamanca scholars based this doctrine firmly on Scripture and natural law, especially as elucidated by St. Thomas Aquinas, himself a Dominican.

In the meantime, Charles had reached Spain. As soon as he arrived at Valladolid in late November, Las Casas and Montesinos pushed to the fore of the petitioners. Humility was not one of the strongest Christian virtues in Las Casas's quiver.

For most of the Christmas season, 1517, and into the early months of winter, 1518, Las Casas plied Charles' largely Flemish advisers with his version of the conquest of the New World. Las Casas did not spare anyone. He pilloried the blindness of the Bishop of Burgos—his old rival Fonseca—and lambasted the people sent by him to govern the Indies.

The Bishop and Secretary Conchillos, Las Casas told Grand Chancellor Jean Sauvage, are destroying the Indies.

"Are they that bad, father?" asked Sauvage.

"Well, one supposes, your grace," Las Casas continued, making a stab at being merciful, "that they didn't *intend* to destroy the Indies with their abysmal administration, and the deaths of so many Indians *may have weighed on them* somewhat."

Sauvage listened, finding the softer side of Las Casas a refreshing break from the customary unrelenting jeremiad. "Nonetheless," Las Casas picked up, "nonetheless, your grace, they cannot be excused from doing *nothing* to change affairs, to remove the causes of such a disaster, to stop the distribution of the Indians, to sack the tyrannical officials, to change to a reasonable and humane way. One supposes," Las Casas added, giving up on his attempt to be charitable and forgiving, "that their own best interests kept them from doing what was right."

While Sauvage listened closely to Las Casas, dozens of powerful *indianos* (or "Indianists," a general term for all conquistadors and settlers personally at the court) pressed for appointments, for legislation, and, equally important to them, for relief from this carping priest and his Dominican supporters. Their arguments were simple. A whole new, and growing, empire was being added to the King's dominions and it was paying thousands of gold pesos into the King's coffers. While the Castilians had to swallow their pride and distaste for the *flamencos*, or Flemings and their foreign-born King, they knew how to appeal to the court: cash. A young King ambitious to become the Emperor of the Holy Roman Empire in an election where votes were very expensive was not unmoved by the appeal to material instincts.

On various occasions Las Casas wrote that Scripture came to mind as he pondered and sought God's will. He frequently salted his rebukes of the *encomenderos* and *indianos* with passages that he easily recalled. "Our Lord himself instructed us your grace, 'No one can serve two masters. Either he will hate the one and love the other, or he will be devoted to the one and despise the other. You cannot serve both God and Mammon.'[9] These men are driven by greed, and all their fine claims to empire and wealth are made on the bodies of Indians."

For a short time in the winter of 1517–1518, Sauvage was swept up by the Lascasian rhetoric. Secretary Conchillos, beseiged by *indianos* demanding that their affairs be addressed, approached Sauvage with a huge bundle of decrees and orders that needed to be signed and dispatched. Conchillos and Fonseca tried to get the King to make the decisions directly, but Charles referred everything to Sauvage. So, reluctantly, Conchillos approached the Chancellor.

"Get out of here," Sauvage snapped at Conchillos. "You and the Bishop have destroyed the Indies."[10]

Conchillos drew back, struck down by the new power at the court. Las Casas's star was rising. Just about every petition submitted by the *indianos* to the court with respect to the Indies now went to Sauvage, and he, in turn, passed it on to Las Casas to review and comment upon. And he loved it. Las Casas translated all the petitions into Latin for the chancellor, and then added a note on what he thought of the content.

"In this way," Las Casas recalled, "I was able to enlighten the chancellor, not only on what was being asked, but on the falsities and lies included, and I brought much light to the things touching on the Indies."

Sauvage in turn told the King about Las Casas. Whether he did so in such flattering terms as Las Casas later recorded in his *History of the Indies* we can only guess.[11] But Charles apparently liked what he heard.

"He speaks the truth, your Majesty," Sauvage told the young King one day, then trying to understand the evolving complexity of his new kingdoms, including the faraway, exotic, and apparently rich, Indies. "Your new subjects, the Indians, are being destroyed by the cupidity of the Castilians. This priest has been there many years. He knows. He has many plans to reform and save what is left from the misrule of your grandfather."

Charles was no admirer of the ruthless King Ferdinand, or of the haughty Castilians he had run into so far. "What to do, Sauvage?" he asked his chancellor.

"Let me get together with the priest and devise a plan, a proposal to deal with this," Sauvage responded. Charles agreed to this and Sauvage informed Las Casas.

Many years later, Las Casas reflected back on that incandescent moment that so lit his life. "And so, for the second time, the livelihood, the liberty, the very lives of the Indians were put in the cleric's hands."[12] Later he recalled bittersweetly, "But later, one way or another, everything fell apart …"

What happened? Here he was at the bustling court of King Charles I of Spain in 1518, soon to be elected Charles V, Holy Roman Emperor, and in the catbird seat of European history, and then "everything fell apart."

Las Casas had two basic plans in mind. While they were different plans, they overlapped in many ways. One was to populate the islands and Tierra Firme with good Spanish farmers. These honest and hardworking souls would transplant the virtues of the Spanish race to the New World, and not engender all the vices of cupidity, brutality, and greed that had so far sprouted like weeds among the settlers and conquistadors. This plan, and all similar ones like it, was born from the recognition that there was no turning back. The discovery, conquest, and settlement of the New World were irreversible. Even if the Spanish could be restrained, their European rivals would not desist. That was the realistic side of Las Casas's nature, although much later in his life he called for the near complete abandonment of the Indies and the restoration or restitution of everything to the Indians.

His second plan was to prohibit entirely, or severely restrict, Spanish settlers of any stripe from further occupying lands and exploiting the native peoples. Only friars and priests would be allowed into the Indies. Endowed with the fruits of the Holy Spirit—love, joy, peace, patience, kindness, goodness, faithfulness—they would then carry the good news of Jesus Christ to Amerindians in peace. This was the only true way to convert pagans or heathen who had never heard the Christian message. In one form or another, combined in certain instances, these two plans became the basis for all of Las Casas's reforms for the Indies.

Las Casas worked feverishly preparing the new plan. The Council of State studied Las Casas's preliminary proposals. Hard-working farmers might be expected to transfer their uplifting values to the Indies. Moreover, the rapidly dwindling Indian population made it expedient to attract more colonists to the new possessions. So, what until then had been a rather helter-skelter process—the migration of Spaniards to the Indies—would now be rationally organized.

While Las Casas vacillated between the two major alternatives, in the end he devised a plan that incorporated both the "good influence" plan with the "exclusion" plan. It led to an unmitigated disaster. In the spring and summer of 1518, however, before all this happened, he was optimistic. If his plans worked, good Spanish farmers might be expected to marry with Indian girls and "together they would make one of the best republics, perhaps the most Christian and peaceful in the world."[13] It was a prophetic vision, but very much in keeping with Las Casas's activist, creative nature. Those who had gone to the Indies up to now—in Las Casas's mind at any rate—were the detritus of humanity, "all types of soulless people who robbed, scandalized, destroyed and laid waste, people who dishonored the name and honor of God with their infamous behavior." The utopian plan was born from his desire to change these circumstances.

There was also a harshly realistic side to this veteran priest who knew the Indies, and was now learning of cupidity at the court. The King was surrounded by counselors who knew the truth (of the rape of the Indies) but were desensitized and subverted by greed. Kings with large ambitions also needed large war chests. Charles badly wanted to win election as Holy Roman Emperor, and that took cash. That was a reality and one Las Casas understood clearly. He realized that he must appeal to the mercenary, as well as spiritual, side of Charles.

In the meantime, another long memorial arrived from the Indies, this time from a Franciscan friar, Francisco de Sant Román, who was with the conquistador Pedrarias Dávila in Panama. "I saw with my own eyes," the Franciscan testified, "forty thousand Indians put to the sword and set upon by fierce war dogs." Sauvage was stupefied by the letter. Las Casas then poured it on. Here was evidence straight from the Indies, objective, simple, truthful, horrible testimony to his own revelations.

"Take that [memorial] to the Bishop [Fonseca], father," Sauvage told Las Casas. Fonseca was ill but Sauvage was angry. "Show it to him. I don't care if he is sick. THAT memorial and what it describes is what is sick." Las Casas took the memorial and read it to Fonseca. The ailing Bishop was no fool. He listened.

"Tell the Chancellor, Father, that I kiss his hands and," he added, "remind him that I already told him it would be good to remove that man [Pedrarias Dávila] from there." Pedrarias had developed a reputation for brutality and fierceness not only with Indians but also against Spanish rivals that made him stand out even among a generation of ruthless conquistadors.

Then Chancellor Sauvage passed away suddenly in early June and Las Casas lost an ally, but it set him back only temporarily. As he remembered with typical perseverance and an unshakable optimism, "the cleric did not faint away from the death of the Grand Chancellor and the other setbacks that afflicted him, for new works arose to challenge him."

After Sauvage's sudden death, Juan [Jean] de Carondolet, the dean of Besançon, was appointed as interim Chancellor. Fat and imperturbable, he did not impress the Protector of the Indians, who resembled a nervous fly around a hippopotamus.

Carondolet fell asleep at Council of State meetings, in spite of Las Casas's efforts to raise his conscience, and sometimes his consciousness as well. Finally one day Carondolet took notice of the scrambling priest around him day and night. "Commendamus in Domino, domine Bartholomee," Carondolet told Las Casas laughingly in Latin, "vestram diligentiam." Or, "We commend your diligence to the Lord, father!"

Other friendships among Charles' courtiers proved fruitful, and as summer gave way to autumn in Zaragoza Las Casas once more rode a crest of optimism. His friends at court promoted his projects, the principal one being the recruitment of Spanish peasants for his immigration project. Las Casas also peppered the Council of the Indies with his petitions as his plans to save the Indies jelled.

A letter from his good friend, the Dominican Pedro de Córdoba still in the Indies, arrived at Zaragoza about this time. The news was awful. Spaniards were raiding all along the Tierra Firme coast, from the island of Trinidad in the east all the way westwards across the coasts of modern Venezuela and Colombia. The search for pearls and slaves were wreaking havoc along the coasts, making the work of Córdoba and his Dominican and Franciscan brothers impossible. "Ask the King for a hundred leagues of Tierra Firme my friend," Córdoba wrote. "Prohibit all the Spaniards except for a few friars. Otherwise all will be lost."

"If you can't get a grant of one hundred leagues," Córdoba pleaded, "then try for ten leagues. If you can't get ten, for God's sake, then negotiate for a few islands off the coast where the friars can tend to those fleeing the persecution of the Spaniards."[14]

"Everything we do," Córdoba explained to one who needed no explanation, "is rendered futile by the acts of those who call themselves 'Christians.'" Father Córdoba's letter inspired Las Casas to a new level of activity. Not only was the preaching of Scripture being undermined, but the very lives of his Dominican and Franciscan friends were also imperiled. So, totally in character, Las Casas took the letter straight to Bishop Fonseca and the Council of the Indies.

The eternal lives of the Indians were being lost by the actions of Spaniards, Las Casas harangued his reluctant listeners. Our friends, such as the godly father Córdoba, are also imperiled by their exposure without any protection. "Our conscience, and the King's conscience," Las Casas continued, ratcheting up his argument, "are heavily weighed by this."

"And what would you have us do, Father?" asked a counselor.

"Why, comply with the wishes of Father Córdoba," Las Casas responded. "Have the King set aside a hundred leagues of Tierra Firme coastline and its interiors where no Spaniards may set foot, except clerics whose only mission is to convert and save souls."

"What is the King to gain," Bishop Fonseca contemptuously shot back, "from granting one hundred leagues to some friars?"

Las Casas was left nearly speechless by the Bishop's mercenary, temporal tone. Fonseca cared not a whit for the saving of souls, a damnable sin given his office of bishop. Scripture leaped into Las Casas's mind. "*Pecunia tua tecum vadad in perditionem.*"[15] He was, for once, truly speechless, not for want of a thought, but for the shock of facing evil so squarely.

Meanwhile, through the good offices of his Flemish friends, Las Casas nonetheless succeeded in getting decrees issued to recruit Spanish peasants to send to the islands. He spent much of the fall, 1518, traveling over parts of Aragon and Castile in northern Spain hunting recruits. Other, disturbing, news was catching up with him that winter of 1518–1519 as well.

One evening he sat down to record his thoughts of those past few weeks, as was his habit, and to read newly arrived letters from the islands. Smallpox is destroying the Indians, he read. Far away on the tropical islands, once lush and filled with a content people, the last of the Indians were dying in misery. On top of this destructive epidemic, a plague of ants swept over the islands of Puerto Rico and Española, devastating the orchards and sugar cane fields now beginning to yield their crops in abundance. There seemed to be little hope of saving the Indians of the islands. Where once there were hundreds of thousands, perhaps millions, now they were being counted in the thousands and even hundreds. They were, in fact, almost totally destroyed by the voracious demands and diseases of the settlers. What next? The mainland, Tierra Firme, was still virgin land, although rapidly being pillaged and tainted by slave raiders and pearl and gold hunters. Father Pedro de Córdoba's plan to set aside an immense swath of land seemed to be the last, great hope.

In the meantime, reports of new, advanced and rich Indian civilizations were circulating through Castile and Aragon, lighting the fires of ambition and adventure, even as the Indians of the islands perished in the holocaust of the Conquest.[16] Hernán Cortés launched his conquest of Mexico in 1519, pushing deep into the Aztec Empire. The immediacy of Las Casas's mission grew with each passing day as letters of newly-discovered Indian peoples and new Indian wealth reached into Spain, all the way from the court of King Charles down to the taverns in the isolated hamlets and towns across the realm. Few were untouched by the gold fever.

Las Casas continued through the fall and into the early winter of 1519 aggressively to lobby for a grant of 1000 leagues of land on the coast of Tierra Firme. Just as surely, Fonseca and others contested him every step of the way, countering his proposals with other, more lucrative plans for the King. Las Casas gradually pared back his request, from 1000 to 600 and finally 300 leagues.

As Las Casas bargained hard for his concessions, he was criticized for his worldliness. One day he was approached by a Licentiate Aguirre, an old timer, probably a Dominican, who had been one of Queen Isabel's executors. Aguirre liked Las Casas, but when he heard the secular provisions of the contract, he balked.

"Father, you have profaned yourself," Aguirre told Las Casas one day outside of the chamber where the council was meeting. Las Casas was aware of critical commentary. Poor old Aguirre stepped into a bear trap.

"How so, Father?"

"Your project, Las Casas. I've heard it is nothing but a commercial enterprise. You have betrayed your evangelical calling," Aguirre sniffed, looking Las Casas straight in the eyes, adding, with disappointment, "I never expected this of you."

"Father," Las Casas began softly. "If you saw our Lord Jesus Christ mistreated, denounced, beaten, injured, and insulted, wouldn't you beg and plead with all your strength to bind him over to you to adore and serve and give him everything any true Christian ought to do?"

"Well, of course."

"And," Las Casas continued, as a tutor to a pupil, even given the great differences in their ages, "if they did not wish to give him over to you, but only to sell him, would you not buy him?"

"Without a doubt, I would buy him."

"Well," and Las Casas dropped the boom, "I have done this, sir. I left Jesus Christ in the Indies, our Lord, lashed, afflicted, beaten, and crucified, not once, but millions of times. That is what the Spaniards are doing in the Indies, the ones who assault and destroy those people, denying

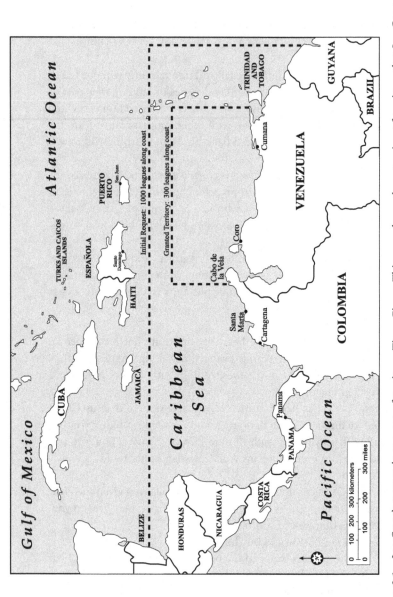

Map 3.1 Las Casas's tremendous grant of territory, Tierra Firme. This map shows the extension of territory that Las Casas eventually received, 300 leagues, an immense piece of the New World reserved in theory for the peaceful occupation of the Americas by Spanish friars and well-meaning farmers.

them conversion and penitence, killing them before their time, and so they die without faith and without sacraments."

Aguirre listened. It was clear where Las Casas was taking him.

"I have pleaded and begged often before the Councils of the King. I have asked for remedy. I have pleaded with them to remove the impediments to salvation. I have asked them to free those taken captive."

"Yes, yes, so I've heard," Aguirre answered. He then tried to defend himself, "but I've heard nonetheless, Father ..."

And now, Las Casas interrupted, "I have asked the council to forbid Spaniards from going to a certain part of Tierra Firme where friars, servants of God, have begun to preach the Gospel. Spaniards who go there, with their violence and bad examples, block the Word of God and blaspheme the name of Christ."

"And the council," Las Casas continued, "has told me that if the friars occupy the land, the King won't get any income." He paused. "You can imagine what their response to my repeated pleas and petitions have been, Father."

"Yes," Aguirre admitted.

"So, you see, when I saw that they wished to sell the Gospel, and Christ, whom they lashed, insulted, and crucified, I decided to buy him, proposing that the King will receive many goods, rents, and riches."

"I see."

"That is what you heard, Father," Las Casas said.

As 1519 drew to a close, Las Casas continued to seek a contract from the Crown for his Tierra Firme experiment. Nonetheless, the roadblocks increased in number and difficulty. Cortés's spectacular discovery of a more complex Amerindian civilization in Mexico fueled gold fever in Spain. Conquistadors were not only pushing into the mainland of Mexico, but also exploring the coastlines, rivers, and estuaries of North and South America.

Exploration and discovery were almost invariably accompanied by conquest and settlement, some successful, some not, but the pace was increasing as the century proceeded. In the fall of 1513, Vasco Núñez de Balboa led a small expedition across the narrow isthmus of Panama and discovered the vast South Sea on September 25, today called the Pacific Ocean. A few months earlier, Juan Ponce de León, a veteran of Columbus's voyages and the conquistador of Puerto Rico, sailed north from Puerto Rico searching for the legendary island of "Bimini" and more Indian slaves to replace the dwindling Taino population of Puerto Rico. On April 2, 1513, he discovered Florida and soon other Spanish explorers were drawing the outline of this vast new continent to the north of Cuba on their maps.

And perhaps the greatest voyage of discovery took place between 1519 and 1521 led by the Portuguese mariner, Ferdinand Magellan, in the service of Spain. He was tasked with sailing south along the South American continent and to find a way through or around that land to the South Sea (Pacific Ocean) and make his way across to China. Magellan in fact did discover a strait (named after him, even today still the "Straits of Magellan") and in a near miraculous voyage of months he crossed the vast Pacific Ocean. Although he died in a skirmish with Philippine Island natives, one of his ships, the *Victoria*, commanded by Juan Sebastián Elcano, made the full circumnavigation of the world, returning to Seville in September, 1522. There were only eighteen survivors of the original crew of 237 in the full fleet that had sailed three years earlier, but they returned with a tale and a reconnaissance of the world unparalleled in the annals of maritime exploration.

So, within a very few years of the first voyage of Columbus, the true dimensions of this vast new world were becoming known to European explorers. And, as these discoveries and explorations proceeded, it became evident that at stake was perhaps even greater wealth and glory than already rendered from the islands in the Caribbean. Were priests and friars (as Las Casas envisioned) to monopolize this cornucopia, a flow of gold and silver that could fill the King's coffers and help Charles realize his dream of a great Christian empire?

Charles was elected Holy Roman Emperor June 28, 1519, while contemporaneously Cortés landed on the coast of Mexico and began his penetration and ultimate conquest of the Aztec Empire with its capital at Tenochtitlan [Mexico City]. To strengthen his position, Cortés had quickly dispatched emissaries—Alonso Hernández de Puertocarrero and Francisco de Montejo—back to Spain.[17] They arrived in Seville in November, carrying the most precious items acquired from early contacts with the Aztecs as gifts for Charles. Puertocarrero and Montejo reached Barcelona by January, 1520, although the news of the fabulous treasure, much gold and beautiful delicate feather work and other fine pieces, traveled faster than they did.

The Emperor, like everyone else, was fascinated with the electrifying news brought by Puertocarrero and Montejo. Solicitations for contracts and patents for further exploration, discovery, and settlement increased as the wealth of the Indies was laid before the very eyes of King and court.

This was the background to Las Casas's ongoing negotiations. Could there be another Aztec empire in the hinterlands of Tierra Firme? So far nothing as grand as Cortés's recent discoveries in Mexico had turned up, but pearls and gold there were aplenty, if not a higher civilization. Who could predict what lay further inland; perhaps El Dorado, the Gilded Man of Gold? In the meantime, Las Casas kept up his drumbeat of truth and justice as near to the face and ears of the King as he could get.

Early in December, 1519, Charles convened a group which included a recent arrival from the Indies, Juan de Quevedo, first Bishop of Darien (Panama), and no friend of Las Casas. Cristobal del Río, a Franciscan, also with experience in the New World, was present, and he greatly admired Las Casas. Charles wanted to hear from all parties.

Bishop Quevedo arrived a little after 11 a.m. for the audience. The King entered and sat on the throne, while the court arrayed itself before him on benches in front of him. All the greats were there: Grand Chancellor Gattinara, Diego Columbus—the son of the Discoverer and the Second Admiral of the Ocean Sea—Bishop Fonseca of Burgos, the Flemings, and others who, Las Casas recalled years later, "have dropped from my memory." Las Casas stood next to the wall facing the King, with the Franciscan del Río beside him.

Gattinara stood up. It was his duty, as the head of all the Councils, to set the agenda and moderate the meeting. "Reverend Bishop," Gattinara said, turning to Bishop Quevedo, "Your Majesty asks that you speak, if you have anything to say about the Indies." Quevedo stood and gracefully bowed before the King.[18]

"Your grandfather," Quevedo started, "the Catholic King [Ferdinand], bless his holy soul, sent a fleet to populate Tierra Firme in the Indies and he asked the Holy Father [Pope] to name me as Bishop for that first settlement. I spent five years in that endeavor, leaving out the days wasted in going over and returning."

This was the expedition of Pedro Arias Dávila (better known as Pedrarias) which was sent by Ferdinand in 1514 with over 2000 men in fifteen ships to settle and exploit the province of Tierra Firme. That section of the coastline had already been explored in part and populated lightly by earlier Spanish conquistadors such as the discoverer of the Pacific, Vasco Núñez de Balboa. The exploits of these early conquistadors were both lucrative and notorious: lucrative for the easy gold and silver extracted from the Amerindians; notorious for the brutal Spanish exploitation of the same Amerindians, especially among the coasts of modern Colombia where it adjoins modern Panama.

Quevedo continued. "As for the Indians, based on my experience and the reports of others, they are born to serve. They have much gold which they esteem. And to obtain it from them, it's necessary to be very industrious." Quevedo finished and sat down. Chièvres and Gattinara consulted with Charles.

"Micer [a corruption of "Monsieur" which Las Casas used in his writings] Las Casas," Gattinara said, turning to Las Casas. "Your Majesty asks you to speak." Las Casas pulled off his clerical bonnet and approached the King. He bowed.

"My Very High and Powerful King and Lord," Las Casas began, and then spoke to establish his credentials. "I am one of the veterans who first traveled to the Indies. I lived there many years. I have seen with my own eyes, not read things in histories which may be untrue. I have touched with my own hands. I have witnessed those gentle and peaceful people suffer monstrous cruelties not even perpetrated in generations past by cruel men or irrational barbarians." Las Casas paused, looking around him, especially at Quevedo, before turning back to Charles.

"And I ask *why*, Your Majesty? Why, without cause or reason, was hell brought alive to these people?"

Charles listened intently.

"Greed, Your Majesty. Unvarnished greed. The thirst and hunger for gold. An insatiable greed that knows no bounds." Then, as a teacher instructs his pupils, as a good advocate prepares his case, Las Casas fleshed out his argument, sensing a breaking moment in his lifelong crusade. Before him was the young King, obviously sympathetic to him. Now Charles needed to be pushed further into the camp of truth and light. He needed to hear, and absorb, the details.

"This has come about in two ways, Your Majesty," Las Casas continued. "One, through the cruel and unjust wars waged on the Indians, people living innocently in their homes and land. There is no telling how many of these people and nations have been killed. Secondly, after having killed the natural lords and principal people, the rest were plunged into servitude. They were divided into lots of a hundred or fifty, forcing them into the mines where they all died from the incredible work of extracting gold."

"All these people, Your Majesty, all," he continued, "perished in these two manners."[19]

"Seeing all this," Las Casas wrote, "I left, not because I was a better Christian than the others, but because of a natural compassion from seeing an innocent people suffer from such grievous assaults and injustices. And so," Las Casas continued, "I came to these kingdoms to tell all this to the Catholic King, your grandfather, then in Placencia. To tell him what I am telling you."

Charles nodded for him to continue.

"Your grandfather received me with kindness and promised to deliver a remedy when in Seville," Las Casas continued his account, "where he was headed. But he died on the journey. After his death, Your Highness, I wrote to those governing the country, the Cardinal of Spain, don Father Francisco Ximenez, and Adrian, now Cardinal of Tortosa. Both were quite well disposed to put a stop to these great injuries so that those people would not perish. But the people [the Hieronymites] sent to execute their orders simply failed to root out such evil and replace it with justice and goodness. So, I am still at work on this, Your Majesty. I do this account of our God, to whom alone all creatures, great and small, owe all honor and glory."

Charles nodded again. The churchmen among the assembled dignitaries, with a few notable exceptions, listened and took comfort from the words of this priest. He was in truth more than a simple priest. Las Casas was indeed a gifted modern prophet, sculpted out of the Old Testament. As it would occur to others over the course of Las Casas's lifetime, Jeremiah came to mind. He spoke the truth, without sugar coating it.

Las Casas's words sank deeply into the heart and soul of the young King, and Charles listened to the Protector of the Indians for the rest of his long reign. It proved to be an extraordinarily solid relationship. It was not, however, always harmonious, for Las Casas sometimes went off the deep end of obsession while Charles had to balance the secular demands of his calling with those of his Christian spirit.

"These people, Your Majesty," Las Casas continued, returning to his theme, firm in his convictions, and confident of his position, "these people who fill the New World are most capable of receiving the Christian faith, of living in virtue with good habits."

Then he moved on to the heart of his defense of Indians that became a refrain in his career. "They are capable of reason, Your Majesty. They are by *nature* [emphasis in the original] free. They have their own kings and natural lords who govern politically."

"As for what the Reverend Bishop said," Las Casas continued, looking at Quevedo sitting on one of the benches behind him, "that these people are by *nature* servants, according to what the Philosopher [Aristotle] wrote in his *Politica:* those who have the capacity to foresee are naturally leaders and lords by their nature; and those who can execute these plans with their bodies are subjects and slaves by nature; well, there's as great a difference as between heaven and earth as between what the Philosopher meant and how the Reverend Bishop took him.[20]

"And, even supposing that it is the way the Reverend Bishop affirms," Las Casas went on, "the Philosopher was a pagan and he is burning in hell." "Anyhow," Las Casas added, "we are too used to invoking his doctrines when it is convenient to support our holy faith and Christian religious customs." So much for Aristotle.

And then, as a preacher to his congregation, or as an exhortation to those about to embark on a mission, Las Casas instructed Charles: "Your Majesty, our Christian religion is for all in the world, and our faith receives the world equally. It does not deprive these people of their liberty or their natural lords, nor does it enslave them under some pretext that they are servile by *nature* as the Reverend Bishop seems to imply."

"What to do, you may be asking, Sire?" Las Casas framed the question for Charles rhetorically. "Right now, at the beginning of your reign, banish the tyranny from those lands that are causing such enormous horror before God and men. Remove those men who are causing such evil and irreparable damage to a major part of the human race, so that the royal Estate of our Lord Jesus Christ, who died for those people, may prosper for many days."

Las Casas stopped. He had talked for 45 minutes. Charles listened closely, as had most of the others in the chamber. When it was apparent that Las Casas's exhortation was finished, Xevres and Gattinara approached the throne to consult quietly with Charles.[21] After a few moments, the King nodded and Gattinara turned to face the chamber. He looked towards the back where the Franciscan del Río stood by the wall.

"Father," Gattinara said, "Your Majesty asks that you speak if you have something to say about matters in the Indies." Del Río stepped forward.

"Sir," Del Rio started, "I was on the island of Española for a number of years. I was ordered to visit and count the number of Indians on that island, and we found there were such and such thousand. After two years, I was ordered to take another census, and we found thousands less who had perished. So, with my own eyes I witnessed the destruction of an infinite number of people on that island." Del Río paused. As a priest and a friar, he knew he had to drive the lesson home for the young King.

"Your Majesty, I beg of you, on the blood of Jesus Christ and the scourges of St. Francis, to remedy such evil condemning those poor souls to perdition each day, I beg of you, Sire, so that God's divine ire won't spill over all of us today!"

Del Río bowed slightly before Charles and returned to sit down next to Las Casas on the bench. Las Casas remembered the scene vividly many years later. That was what the religious Franciscan father said, Las Casas recalled. It was brief, he wrote, but he said everything so vividly and with such fervor that it seemed all who were there were already standing before the Final Judgment.[22]

At stake here was not only the fate of millions, but also, more immediately, the mind, and soul of the young King Charles. Las Casas, following the lead of del Río and other impassioned friars, raised the stakes in this endeavor to the penultimate level—eternal life or eternal fire after death. The King's soul was at stake, and it was a trump card that Las Casas played often in the coming decades. He liked the young King Charles, and the fondness was reciprocated.

When del Río turned to sit down, Xevres and Gattinara approached the throne once again, exchanging a few whispers.

"Your Majesty," Bishop Quevedo then stood up, "may I speak?"

Xevres, Gattinara and the King consulted. Gattinara turned around. "Reverend Bishop," the Grand Chancellor said, "His Majesty says if you have more to say, put it in writing."

The King rose and took his leave. That ended the session. It was the most important audience of Las Casas's life, for he had secured a line to Charles' spirit and conscience that remained strong throughout the lives of both men.

As Christmas Eve, 1519, neared, the King and his councilors grew even warmer in their sentiments for "Micer" Las Casas. It was not simply a measure of Las Casas's persistence, or of the camaraderie that flourished between the King and the priest. His message was powerful. It was of salvation in the next world, as much as of the need to save the Indians in this world. The two were inextricably bound, as the Franciscan del Río had so vividly linked them during the audience of December 12.

The King left Barcelona for the port of La Coruña on the Bay of Biscay late in January, 1520. Having been elected Holy Roman Emperor, Charles was bound for Flanders and Germany to be crowned. He departed La Coruña on May 19, 1520, in a fleet of almost 100 vessels appropriate to his rank and the importance of the trip. Bishop Fonseca, now back in the good graces of the court, was in charge.

On his slow journey across northern Spain to La Coruña, Charles saw some of the wealth of the Indies with his own eyes. Hernán Cortés's emissaries, Montejo and Puertocarrero, finally caught up with the king in Valladolid. The display of Aztec treasure was breathtaking. In a decision that proved fatal, the Aztec Emperor Moctezuma had hoped to turn away with gifts the invading Spanish army camped on the flanks of his empire around Veracruz. It was an error of judgment that cost him dearly. The treasure only whetted the appetites of the Spaniards who under the brilliant leadership of Cortés pushed into the interior of Mexico, defeating Aztec allies, arriving at Tenochtitlán (today Mexico City) in November, 1519. The defeat and plunder of the capital of the Aztecs went on for two years (see next chapter), producing even more spectacular wealth than that sent by Cortés to King Charles in the early stages of the conquest of Mexico.

The King was duly impressed with the gifts which included fabulous works of gold, silver, weaving, and art work. They testified to a more

Figure 3.1 "The Tlascalans Suing for Peace with Cortés." Source: From Diego Durán (1537–1588), a Dominican friar, like Las Casas, who wrote one of the earliest, sympathetic, books (*The History of the Indies of New Spain*, 1581) on the history and culture of the Aztecs. Fluent in Nahuatl, the Aztec language, he incorporated much of Aztec lore and images into his works.

complex civilization, far above and far different from the village level native peoples of the Caribbean islands. Two massive "wheels," as Las Casas described them, occupied center stage. One of was of gold with a representation of the sun, the other of silver with the figure of the moon. They were as large as the wheels of a carriage, as thick as a man's arm. Even the pious Flemings who sided with Las Casas in his battles against the greedy Spaniards had to admit that this display was a most impressive testament to the increasing value of the Indies. There might be many souls to save indeed, but there appeared to be as much gold to get as souls to save.

Las Casas saw it also with his own eyes.[23] He was impressed, as everyone else, by the magnificence of the treasure. He also saw the lights of greed flicker to life in the eyes of all who witnessed the display. So much gold. How it transforms a man's nature!

Las Casas followed the court to La Coruña in late March where Charles resided as the fleet prepared to sail. The last seven days before the fleet sailed on May 19 were marked by feverish activity. All of the councils—of State, of the Indies, and so on—met daily to transact business before Charles departed. Cardinal Adrian, soon to be elevated to the Papacy, brought some closure to where Charles and he—as regent in the King's forthcoming absence—stood on Las Casas and matters of the Indies.

For Las Casas this was essential, for the criticism of the Indianists at the court was constant and, from a material perspective, very persuasive. They claimed they would lose their livelihood if the *encomienda*s were ended or abridged. They argued that the King's present and future revenues would be depleted by any attempts to put friars where good Spanish citizens (read conquistadors and slavers) could and should spread the fruits of Spanish civilization and sovereignty. Savages, cannibals, and pagans most certainly could be converted only after submitting to secular authority.

In a session attended by the leading members of the court only days before Charles sailed, Adrian delivered a learned discourse. The Cardinal, steeped in humanism and a scholar of rank, drew deeply from canon law, natural law, Scripture, and the Church fathers for his arguments. It was a *tour de force*.

"These people," he told his listeners, "can be brought to the knowledge of God and the brotherhood of our Holy Church only by peace and love and the evangelical way taught by Christ."

It was hard to argue with such a broad definition of Christian evangelism based on love, the building block of the Christian faith.

"We cannot wage war on them and enslave them," Adrian continued.

He knew the proud Spanish tradition, the story of the long Reconquest of Iberia for Christendom over the Muslims. Many of the faces before him had known the age of Isabel and Ferdinand, had slain Moors in the name of the Faith, and marched triumphantly with their Catholic Sovereigns into mighty Granada in 1492.

But Adrian rejected the way of war: "We cannot follow the way of Muhammed and be images of our Lord Jesus Christ."[24]

What was the reaction to this condemnation of the "Muhammedan way," as Las Casas recalled it? "So powerful was the oration of the saintly cardinal," Las Casas remembered, "that all, or, most at any rate, approved of and praised his Catholic doctrine."

HADRIANVS VI. PONT. MAX.
Edit Vtricesium minimo de fomite lucem,
Lampada Louanium, Roma dat esse Pharum.
Fax animæ cineri nimium est vicina dolofo,
Et quæ lentè oritur flamma, cito emoritur.
Disce meo exemplo tenui de lumine Solem
Sperare, et Solis difce timere obitum.

Figure 3.2 Pope Adrian VI, 1522–523, Las Casas's ally for many years when Adrian helped rule Castile, first as co-regent with Cardinal Cisneros in 1516–1517, and then in 1520 as regent when the Emperor Charles V returned to Flanders in May, 1520, on his way to being crowned Holy Roman Emperor.

The Indians, Adrian ended, should be free, and should be treated as free individuals, to be brought to the Faith by the way left for us by Christ. This perfectly summarized Las Casas's principal thesis. The Indians are free. From that premise, all other conclusions and disputes flowed, everything from the right of the Spanish even to be in the New World, to the nature of man, itself a battleground between Christian doctrine and pagan scholarship, largely derived from Aristotle.

Charles signed Las Casas's grant of territory on May 19, 1520, on the very eve of his departure from La Coruña. It was not what Las Casas proposed initially. His thousand leagues had been carved back by Fonseca and the Indianists to less than three hundred. The Indians to the east and west of his grant would be threatened. No matter. Las Casas had his grant. Soon after the King and his galleons set sail, Las Casas turned south for his hometown of Seville to prepare to sail to the Indies once again.

4

The Era of the Conquests of Mexico and Peru, 1520s–1540s

Seville, autumn, 1520

Once again Las Casas was riding a high tide. When the Emperor Charles signed off on his contract to settle Tierra Firme, Las Casas had his marching orders for reform. Although pared back by Fonseca and his allies, Las Casas's grant was still immense. It covered 270 leagues from the Paria Peninsula in the east to near Santa Marta in the west. See Map 3.1 for the approximate region covered by the grant.

Inland, Las Casas's grant ran to more than two thousand leagues, or virtually the entirety of the continent of South America. Even given his disappointment at not obtaining the full thousand leagues, or more than three thousand miles of coastline, the grant was spectacular.

After the departure of the king and his court, Las Casas traveled to Seville where he arrived sometime late in the summer of 1520, armed with letters from the regent Adrian and other influential churchmen. With almost a hundred recruits he had picked up along the way, he boarded the small fleet of three vessels that dropped down the Guadalquiver River the first week of December. They crossed the bar at Sanlúcar de Barrameda on December 14 and set sail for Puerto Rico.[1] The voyage was good, and swift. They dropped anchor in the harbor of San Juan about a month later, or the middle of January, 1521.

Bartolomé de las Casas and the Conquest of the Americas. Lawrence A. Clayton
© 2011 Lawrence A. Clayton

"What's new?!" hailed the sailors from the ships as boats from the harbor master went out to greet them.

"Good news! Indians in rebellion!" the rowers shouted back as they neared the ships having just crossed the Atlantic.

"Indians in rebellion? Good news?"

Las Casas flashed back to 1502, almost two decades earlier, when he arrived in the Indies for the first time.

The news was good then also. Indians in rebellion! This meant that one could make war on them legally to restore them to Spanish authority, and to enslave them legally.

The old nightmare crossed Las Casas's horizon as he disembarked and hurried to see Antonio de la Gama, the Chief Justice of Puerto Rico who had just completed a special investigation for the Crown on the island. In the meantime, while Las Casas launched his second great experiment in settling the Indies and social planning, Cortés was waging a hotly contested war against the Aztecs of Mexico.

The conquest of Mexico

The conquest of Mexico is the focal point of the Spanish invasion of the New World. It set the mark for the Spaniards.[2] It has long been seen as testimony to the magnificent feats of arms by a handful of Spanish warriors in the midst of an Amerindian empire of millions in the heart of Mexico. Cortés led an expedition of about 550 men to the coast of Mexico in 1519 and in the space of two years he conquered tens of thousands of warriors in the combined armies of the Aztecs and their allies.

Modern research has altered this view somewhat.[3] It turns out that "General Smallpox," or the role of diseases in undermining both the will and the substance of the Aztec resistance to the invasion, especially of the Aztec capital of Tenochtitlán which the Spanish first entered on November 8, 1519, played at least an equal role in determining the winners and losers in this titanic struggle for triumph or survival (depending on your point of view) in the central valley of Mexico.

Second, the role of the Aztec tributary peoples—those conquered by the Aztecs—played an immense role in the defeat of the Aztecs. Once defeated by Cortés, they turned into very willing allies, using the Spanish to make war on their old enemies and conquerors, the Aztecs themselves. "The conquest," wrote one historian, "was more like an internal revolution against Aztec rule than a European invasion of an Amerindian state."[4]

Third, the Aztecs gave as much as they took, almost wiping out the invading Spanish army camped in the capital of Tenochtitlán on July 1, 1520. Much vaunted Spanish technological superiority—Toledan steel over Aztec wooden clubs, for example—failed dismally to preserve the Spanish who were driven out of the city by Aztec warriors confirming what another close student of the conquest of Mexico wrote: "I would argue that the final conquest was a very close-run thing."[5] Other traditional interpretations of this two-year running battle between the invading Spaniards and the defending Aztecs have been equally questioned by a closer reading of the sources by modern scholars.

Some traditional accounts—based on Spanish chronicles of the conquest of Mexico written at the time, or by contemporaries, for example, claimed the Indians thought perhaps the Spaniards were godlike, semidivine creatures, and, according to Mexican myths, returning to claim their inheritance. This threw the Aztecs, and especially their emperor, Moctezuma, into a paralysis of sorts that led to indecision at crucial junctures of the campaign. But Aztec warriors, and their allies, soon discovered that Spanish warriors bled and died just like them and the horses were not invulnerable animals. Cut their tendons or hooves and they were crippled and could be maimed or killed.

So why *did* the Spanish finally triumph over the Aztecs in the conquest of Mexico? In the annals of military history, it was a unique event. An invading army that fluctuated in size from several hundred to one or two thousand eventually brought an empire with tens of thousands of warriors to their knees, and finally to surrender. And the conquest of Mexico confirmed the tone of superiority, if not invincibility, of Spanish men at arms in the making of the Spanish empire in the Indies. There were reverses and occasional Spanish defeats—some disastrous, and great victories for Amerindians—but these were the exception, not the rule. The imposition of Spanish rule brought with it Spanish laws, customs, language, habits of work and life, domestic relations, political structures, and the Spanish religion that inexorably produced a new civilization in the Indies based on the encounter with Amerindian cultures. But the tone was set for the next three centuries. One culture—the Amerindian—was considered subservient or inferior to the other—the Spanish—because the triumph of arms made it so. That is the way Cortés and most of his contemporaries viewed their destiny as they crafted it.

The Conquest itself took over two years and is complicated, and fascinating. Very briefly, here is what happened. Cortés came to the Indies in 1504, only two years after Las Casas, but under slightly different circumstances.[6] Cortés's life paralleled Las Casas in many ways. They were the same age, both born in 1485. They both first went to Santo Domingo, and later Cortés joined Velázquez on his conquest of Cuba that began in 1511. That is where the parallel tracks of these two seminal figures in the Conquest began to grow apart. While Las Casas had his epiphany at the massacre of Caonao in 1514, Cortés led an expedition of conquest to the coast of Mexico in early 1519, where he overcame initial Amerindian resistance, founded a city at Veracruz, and began overtures to the emperor Moctezuma still at his capital in Tenochtitlán two hundred miles away.

The story here gets complicated, and has been retold in hundreds of books since then. Basically, we need to be cognizant of three distinct points of view: first, that being formed by Las Casas and his allies then—in 1519—petitioning the King for the right to evangelize Tierra Firme exclusively; second, the one of Cortés and his army of soldiers-of-fortune who told Moctezuma's emissaries that the Spaniards suffered from a disease of the heart only curable by gold; and, third, the perspective of Moctezuma, the ruling Aztecs, and the subject peoples they themselves had only conquered in the past century.

When Cortés led his army away from the coast and into the interior towards the Aztec capital, he made use of several strategic and tactical advantages, most of which he had some control over, some of which circumstances simply threw into his lap. He used his technological superiority well, especially the ability to move swiftly with his cavalry and use his horses to great effect in battle. Just the roar of cannon muzzles, accompanied by fire and smoke, and the devastating effect of cannon balls tended to intimidate Amerindian warriors facing such weaponry for the first time.

Equally important—perhaps more so in the final reckoning—were the Indian allies Cortés picked up along his march into the interior. Indian peoples—such as the Totonacs and Tlaxcalans—had been conquered themselves by the expanding Aztec empire and, after some initial resistance to the Spanish, they viewed the Spanish as allies in overthrowing Aztec rule. They proved to be formidable allies when one considers the disproportionate numbers involved if one were to consider simply Spaniards against the Aztecs.

There were other factors at work. Some students of the Conquest/ Encounter give the Spanish ability to write and communicate the edge. Others have identified the innate weakness of the Aztecs, who were accustomed to something loosely labeled "ceremonial" war, or warfare made simply for cultural and religious reasons, as opposed to the Spanish concept of war, not only to the death, but for ultimate victory and dominance.[7] And the role of disease cannot be underestimated. When Cortés and his army were at a low point in the campaign in 1521, beaten it seemed and on the retreat, "General Smallpox" came marching in, as you will see below.

Among those elements that have to be reckoned with in any historical account was the nature of the people involved. Did a Cortés or a Moctezuma, by their valor or cowardice, by their ambition or ambivalence, by their very nature, affect the outcome more so, for example, than the circumstances surrounding the campaign—such as technology, mobility, disease, alliances, translators, cultural misunderstandings, and the like? Do powerful individuals make history, or are they simply pushed along by great tides of political, religious, social, and economic forces in the affairs of humans?

At the center of this historic encounter was of course Cortés, and he seemed to have emerged either providentially, if one was a good Spanish Catholic believing in the ultimate triumph of God, or as an awful destiny ordered by offended gods and deities in the Aztec cosmos which governed the relationship between humans and the divine.

At the core of Cortés's existence was a profound faith that sustained him through his life. In this, he shared a quality with Las Casas. And curiously, because each suspected the other's motives and actions over the years, and certainly were not friendly, they shared an intense commitment to spreading the faith. Las Casas came to the conclusion that it could only be legitimately done by peaceful persuasion and love, a philosophy which drove his first book written in the 1530s, *The Only Way*. Cortés, faced with human sacrifices on a grotesque scale and other barbarities associated with pagan worship within the Aztec empire, dealt with it directly, destroying idols, smashing temples and inculcating the rudiments of Christianity with a passion.[8]

And, even more coincidentally, both Las Casas and Cortés viewed the Spanish presence in the islands of the Caribbean as disastrous. Cortés was devoted to bringing Amerindians to the one true faith and also creating an empire for Castile. "But there was a wrong way," as J. H. Elliott wrote, "as well as a right way, of going about this great work."[9] Both had witnessed how "captains and soldiers whose sole concern was the quest for gold and the capture of slaves and booty had destroyed the islands and people discovered by Columbus only a generation ago."[10] Cortés had as a goal to build a colony in the growing empire of the king, not just pillage and loot. But first, of course, he had to win the empire.

When he turned inland in the fall of 1519, he made his way to the city of Cholula in the highlands. There, in an act of treachery or from astute intelligence, he massacred more than 6000 Cholulan warriors whom he suspected of setting an ambush for the Spaniards. The devastating defeat of the Cholulans, allies of the Aztecs, stunned Moctezuma in his capital at Tenochtitlán, not sure of how to deal with this invading army.

What was Moctezuma thinking as he received reports of the seemingly inexorable advance of this invading army, so strange in its appearance, its behavior, and so difficult to deal with? He sent gifts and envoys and politely asked them to leave. But they kept coming. He incited his allies to attack them. They did, and like the Cholulans, were blasted by cannon and skewered by swords and lances, into utter defeat. And then, to worsen matters, some like the Tlaxcalans, joined the Spaniards by the thousands, adding warriors with no love of the Aztecs who in the past had taken Tlaxcalans, and other peoples, captive, brought them to Tenochtitlán, and ritually sacrificed them by tearing their hearts out.

On November 8, 1519, Cortés entered the capital and was greeted by Moctezuma formally. There ensued an awkward period of about six months during which the Spanish were not sure whether they had occupied a city, or were themselves the captives, surrounded by thousands of warriors. In a preemptive strike so characteristic of the bold Spanish captain, Cortés took Moctezuma prisoner and held him hostage in his own palace, although treating him with the greatest respect. The Spaniards—shocked by the signs of pagan worship—continued smashing idols and insisting that human sacrifices cease. Only one God reigned and so the signs of Christianity—crosses, images of the Virgin Mary—were introduced. None of this—the capture of their emperor, the destruction of their religious symbols and prohibition of worship, the presence of an invading army—sat well with Moctezuma's warrior nobility. Then Moctezuma's gods seemed to have intervened. A sizable force (bigger than Cortés army in Mexico) commanded by Pánfilo de Narváez had landed on the coast, bent on arresting Cortés and bringing him to justice for an earlier altercation with the Governor of Cuba, Diego de Velázquez, who considered Cortés a rebel for disobeying his orders.[11] Cortés hurried to the coast with a small force, dividing his army, leaving Pedro de Alvarado in Tenochtitlán. Perhaps the Spanish would destroy each other in civil war! Is this what Moctezuma thought? His intelligence was excellent and he followed the movements of the Spaniards with concentration. His life and the existence of his empire apparently depended more and more on the invaders.

But Cortés defeated Narváez in a surprise night attack, and, against overwhelming odds, forced Narváez to surrender and persuaded most of his men to join him. When Cortés returned to Tenochtitlán in June 1520, he found an edgy city in rebellion against Alvarado who—in Cortes's absence—had sprung a surprise attack on Aztec nobles and warriors in the central plaza, slaughtering hundreds and driving the Aztecs to revenge. Even with over a thousand soldiers and a hundred cavalry to reinforce Alvarado's besieged forces, the Aztec assault on the Spanish was driven by anger, fury, and overwhelming forces. Moctezuma was killed in the battle, whether by his own people or the Spanish is forever lost in the mist of conflicting evidence. The Spanish retreated with heavy losses, over 450 men killed and dozens captured, later to be sacrificed by the Aztecs. But retreat, no matter how humiliating and demoralizing, only seemed to harden Cortés's resolve, and his Indian allies stood by him as he regrouped and prepared to return for a final assault on Tenochtitlán. It began in December, 1520, and lasted more than six months, including savage hand-to-hand fighting in the later stages of the campaign, as the Aztec warriors fought to the death and Cortés, unable to bring them to surrender, methodically destroyed the city and slaughtered the defenders.

And smallpox made its first appearance in Mexico as well. The disease, unknown in the Americas, arrived with some of Narváez's men, and it spread quickly, killing tens of thousands of Aztecs, undermining the will to resist just when they needed it most. Moctezuma's nephew Cuauhtémoc, who was elected as emperor after his uncle perished, surrendered after leading a valiant defense, and he is still considered a hero in Mexico today.

Cortés's victory opened a new era in the conquest of the Americas. Spanish armies—mostly small but very effective—moved through the more complex state-level peoples first of Mexico, then down through the Maya of southern Mexico, the Yucatán peninsula and into Central America in the 1520s and 1530s, and finally drove down into South America, into the heart of the Inca Empire in the 1530s and 1540s, each instance of conquest establishing with greater firmness Spain's growing empire in the Indies. While Cortés led this epic conquest like a dagger into the heart of the Aztecs and laid the foundations for a new state in Mexico built on loyalty to the Spanish crown, the lordship of Spaniards over Aztecs, and firmly grounded in the Church, Las Casas was waging his own battle against the very ferocity of Spaniards that characterized the conquest of Mexico.

While he knew Cortés, and had seen with his own eyes the treasure Cortés's emissaries had shown to Charles and his court early in 1521, Las Casas was on his own mission, to save the Indians of Tierra Firme. Those Indians had risen in revolt and destroyed the Dominican outpost at Chiribichi on the eastern coastline of modern Venezuela, in the province of Cumaná. They threatened a Franciscan mission nearby at Cumaná. Worst of all, a punitive expedition had been launched from Santo Domingo, led by Gonzalo de Ocampo, to sail to the coast of Tierra Firme and crush the rebellion.[12]

Everyone knew the consequences. Indians in rebellion meant Indians to be enslaved, legally and with the consent of all involved, except, of course, for a few wild-eyed radicals like the priest Bartolomé de las Casas, only recently arrived in Santo Domingo with his commissions and grants from the Crown. Try as he might, Las Casas failed to stop Ocampo's punitive slave raiding expedition.

Las Casas waved around his orders from the King and Council. Ocampo and others in charge ignored them. The King was far away. This was the Indies, and Ocampo had his orders from the Audiencia (or governing council) of Santo Domingo.

Ocampo was invoking a new strategy for the New World. While he acknowledged the authority of Las Casas's commissions and recognized the authority of the Crown, he patently disobeyed them. He invoked a principle summarized by the phrase *obedezco pero no cumplo* [*I obey but do not comply*]. This became a standard way of expressing general loyalty to the Crown, but manifestly rejecting the validity of any particular decree, order, or commission related to administering the Indies.

It sounds strange to modern ears. How can one obey and not comply? The key to this odd-sounding phrase and practice lay first in the vast distances between Spain and the Indies, and, second, in the independent nature of the Spanish conquistador. To Las Casas, it was simple disobedience and insubordination. To Ocampo, it was good sense. He was in the Indies, Charles I was back in Spain, maybe even far off in the Lowlands or Germany. From such a distance, the concepts of authority and obedience were mere principles. Loyalty to the Emperor was professed but, in this particular instance, obedience made no practical sense. Besides, there was money to be made in the slave trade.

This small—though certainly not unimportant—incident was emblematic of the challenge of governing the Indies from Spain. Spaniards marching through the mountains and plains and islands of the New World were no less Spaniards there than back in Castile or Aragón. But they were separated by a vast gulf of geographic distance, and were thrust into the role of independent entrepreneurs and soldiers, betting their lives and their fortunes that they could conquer and settle this strange new land and its peoples.

Their point of view was distinctly different from that of the King and his bureaucrats back in Spain. The King demanded loyalty and obedience and taxes while the conquistadors viewed royal authority as intrusive, usurping what they won in battle by their blood and sacrifice. In this instance, Las Casas came armed with royal edicts; Ocampo, on the other hand, was armed with his own ships and soldiers. The contest was between power—Ocampo—and obedience to the Crown—Las Casas.

Ocampo's ships from his punitive expedition to Tierra Firme returned a month or so later, loaded with Indian slaves. Las Casas's rage crested like a wave, due not only to the sight of the pitiful Indian slaves, but also as he heard of Ocampo's acts on the coast—*his* coast by grant of the King of Spain and the Emperor of the Holy Roman Empire![13]

When Ocampo's pitiful cargo of Amerindian slaves was unloaded on the dock at Santo Domingo, Las Casas—who had sailed to Santo Domingo from Puerto Rico in the meantime—lost his ecclesiastical demeanor.

He immediately called on the Audiencia and denounced Ocampo as a detestable tyrant. After being dressed down by Las Casas, the judges of the Audiencia came up with a plan to reconcile the priest who came armed with royal grants with the reality of life in the Indies. They created a "company" to settle Tierra Firme, toning down the ecclesiastical nature of the enterprise with some "good sense" profit-sharing elements to the project.

Years later, he remembered what he did: "So seeing there was no other way to get to the mainland, that the only way he could get there was with the good will and resources of those proposing this 'company,' that meanwhile they would continue to depopulate and ravage the land, enslaving its people, agreed to the terms and said he would be pleased to join the company."[14]

It was a bad bargain. Yet, he was almost out of resources. He could not even get to Tierra Firme on his own. He had no choice and entered into an agreement with them.[15] He thought he could control the insatiable greed for pearls and gold, and, in exchange, somehow suppress the slave trade. He was wrong. The next two years were disastrous for him.

The title of Chapter 158 in Book III of his *History of the Indies* does little to sugarcoat the results: "The Voyage of the Cleric Casas to Cumaná and the Disaster Which Ensued." He went to Cumaná and struggled to keep alive the spirit of the small Dominican and Franciscan settlements in the face of the cupidity and greed of Spanish slavers along the coast, but in the end the Indians turned on the missionaries as but another face of the invaders and slavers. Unable to keep secular Spaniards off the coast, Las Casas, urged by his fellow friars, returned to Santo Domingo in late 1521 to deal with his enemies. While Las Casas was on the voyage back to Santo Domingo, the Indians revolted, destroying both the Franciscan and a small Dominican mission, making smoke and ashes of Las Casas's dreams.

Before Las Casas arrived back at Santo Domingo, the rumors that he had died in the Indian uprising spread around the capital. "This news pleased many," Las Casas recorded dryly in his *History*, "and few were displeased."[16] Las Casas was dead! On with the slave raids!

Father Las Casas was, however, walking back through the mountains of central Española on his way back to Santo Domingo after the pilot of his ship had mistakenly landed on the far west of the island. One afternoon, by the rushing waters of a cool river, Las Casas stopped to take a nap with his small retinue. Some travelers going in the opposite direction happened by.

"Hey, what's the news in Santo Domingo, of Spain? We've been away a long time," Las Casas's companions asked.

"Well, not much," the other travelers answered, sitting down to share the shade of the large trees and rest from the heat of the day. "The Indians of the Pearl Coast killed the priest Bartolomé de las Casas and all his family. Not much else going on."

"What! That's impossible!"

"What do you mean impossible? The news came straight from the survivors. He's dead."

While they argued, Las Casas woke up from a deep sleep. He listened for a while to their sharp words.

"Father Las Casas is over there sleeping. He's not dead!"

"What?"

Las Casas felt himself slowly rising as from a deep abyss. "Dead? Maybe I am dead. Everything I've worked for is gone and lost. I joined with those driven by greed to make this company work. And now it's dead. I offended God by confusing a truly pure and spiritual work with the garbage and worldly lusts of man. I trusted in a company of gentlemen entrepreneurs and royal officials to make this expedition to Tierra Firme possible."

"I have grown so far from Jesus Christ," he thought, lying there listening as the travelers debated his death.[17]

After the rest stop, the small entourage resumed its journey across the mountains and rivers to the capital at Santo Domingo where they arrived, March 18, 1522. It was with a heavy heart that they heard the news of Cumaná. The same travelers who had reported Las Casas's somewhat premature demise also brought news of the subsequent attack by the Indians, the deaths of four Spaniards, and the abandonment of the missions.

Depressed by his circumstances, Las Casas was taken in warmly by the Dominicans in Santo Domingo, notably among them Father Domingo de Betanzos.

"Why don't you join us?" Betanzos urged Las Casas over the next few months. "You have worked hard on behalf of the Indians, Father. Now that such a pious work has failed, perhaps it is God's way of telling you not to follow that path."

Betanzos worked on the reluctant, but listening Las Casas. "Let the secular people colonize, Father. Our mission is not to settle, not to found, not to colonize, not to govern. No, Father, ours is to preach the Word, to exhort, to reproach, to instruct." Las Casas finally yielded and asked Betanzos in 1522 to begin his initiation into the Order of Preachers, the Dominicans.

The Dominican community was elated. Indeed, everyone in the Indies seemed happy with this decision: "[T]he friars, spiritually, for the conversion of one they loved; and the others because the one who thwarted their robberies and constantly interrupted their sinful temporal interests was now to be buried in a monastery."

So early in 1523, around March, Las Casas was formally initiated as a Dominican novice in Santo Domingo. Las Casas renounced the world he had inhabited and went into a metaphorical "sleep," as he himself described it.[18] He turned away from the tug of the world of action to the tranquility of the monastery.

But "sleep" to one man is quite different to another. From 1523 to about 1526, he devoted himself to the agenda set for him by his Dominican brothers in Santo Domingo. He dug into the books of the great Church Fathers, read the ancient pagan philosophers, and immersed himself in Scripture. He reflected on his life, his faith, and the principles of Christianity measured against the reality of the ongoing conquest and colonization of the New World.

Then, in 1527, he was given a new task. Las Casas's superiors sent him to the north coastal town of Puerto de Plata facing the Atlantic Ocean, to found a Dominican house. There he built a small stone monastery, planted a garden, and, in the quiet and fertile peace of the small port, he also began to compile and write his *History of the Indies*, a work of monumental proportions that occupied him—off and on—for the rest of his life. As he began to emerge from his self-described long "sleep" in the early 1530s, the Spanish conquest of the Americas was picking up momentum.

In 1534, the news that Francisco Pizarro had extracted a fabulous ransom in gold and silver from the Inca Emperor Atahualpa in Peru spread through the empire, and the race of Spaniards to Peru was on. The news of the treasure of the Incas traveled through the towns and cities of Spain and the Indies like an elixir.

The similarities between the conquest of Peru and the earlier conquest of Mexico were many, including the role of diseases, divisions among the Incas, a small Spanish army in the midst of warriors in the tens of thousands, technology, religious omens, and even the backgrounds of the conquistadors, both Cortés and Pizarro coming from the hardscrabble province of Extremadura in Spain. Pizarro had actually come over to the Indies on the same fleet with Las Casas in 1502 and lived on the island some time before emerging as a leading conquistador in the subjugation of Panama in the second decade of the sixteenth century. An experienced and ambitious Indian fighter, he then spent much of the 1520s in exploratory expeditions from Panama down the west coast of South America, searching for a legendary land of gold and riches named Biru or Piru. As luck or providence would have it, he found it in 1532 when he entered the northern reaches of the Inca empire and discovered an Amerindian empire as rich as that discovered by his countryman Cortés just a little over a decade before in Mexico.

The Inca empire covered most of Peru, much of modern Bolivia, Ecuador, and parts of modern Chile, and through alliances and trade, it even reached into modern Colombia and Argentina, a truly immense and rich empire. When Pizarro and his very small army of 106 foot soldiers and 62 cavalry entered the highland city of Cajamarca in northern Peru, like Cortés before him in Tenochtitlán, Pizarro was not sure whether he was surrounded or had been given the opportunity of a lifetime. It turned out to be the latter, at least from the perspective or point of view of the invaders.

The emperor of the Incas, Atahualpa, was surrounded by an army of thousands of Inca warriors who had emerged victorious in a civil war between Atahualpa and his brother Huascar.[19] He feared no one, especially this small group of men and horses—no matter how novel their presence was in the Andean world of the Inca. The kingdom divided between warring brothers may have been a legacy from smallpox or some other plague that killed their father Manco Capac around 1526.

Pizarro seized Atahualpa in November, 1532 in a bold ambush set right in the middle of Cajamarca, and subsequently trumped up charges of polygamy, incestuous marriage, and idolatry, and had Atahualpa executed in August, 1533.[20] Prior to that, Atahualpa, held as hostage, had sent for enough gold and silver in his kingdom to fill a room in Cajamarca. When the objects were melted down into bars and ingots, each man received a percentage based on his rank and investment in the campaign.

From Cajamarca, Pizarro and the main body of the Spanish army penetrated into the very heart of the Inca Empire and captured the capital of Cuzco in November, 1533. An orgy of looting and pillaging followed, and in 1535 this phase of the conquest of Peru ended with the founding of the Spanish city of Lima on the coast.

The effect of Pizarro's *entrada* (armed expedition, often used to denote the invasion of Spanish armies—large or small) was like an explosion amidst the Incas and the many other Amerindian peoples of the world set high in the cordilleras of the Andes and scattered along the river oases on the desert coastline of much of Peru. Many of them were no friends of the Incas, and they willingly joined the Spanish as allies. Others had been defeated supporting Atahualpa's rival in the civil war and they too viewed the Spanish as liberators of sorts, who could be manipulated. Civil war broke out among the Spaniards themselves over the spoils of the conquest of Peru, and Pizarro was assassinated in 1541 by the son of a rival. Remnants of the Inca nobility escaped into the high jungles of the eastern Andes and held out until the 1570s. But the seemingly inexorable triumph of Spanish arms, accompanied by the usual devastating diseases such as measles and smallpox, and the rapid increase in the European population in the second half of the sixteenth century eclipsed, but did not extinguish, the Incas. Even though demographers have estimated that maybe as much as 80–90 percent of the Amerindian population of Peru was gone by the end of the century, hundreds of thousands survived and started to adapt to the imposition of an alien culture and conqueror.

Map 4.1 The Route of the Conquistadors into Peru. Led by Francisco Pizarro, a small Spanish army of less than 200 men captured the Inca Emperor Atahualpa in 1532, precipitating the conquest of the Incas.

Meanwhile, the news of the Incas and of their fabulous wealth had exploded across the growing Spanish empire in the New World in 1533 and 1534. Ever the preacher, and perhaps a bit self-righteously, Las Casas pointed out the vast difference that lay between the wealth of the Inca and the wealth of the true Christian.

"And neither your Excellencies, nor Your Majesty," Las Casas wrote to the Council of the Indies and Emperor Charles, "should revel in the apparent riches from Peru, no matter how enormous they may seem."

The preacher in Las Casas rose to the occasion: "No, I tell you truthfully that there are more and better riches which Your Majesty may claim by another, more just, way, and that is through the way of evangelism, the very way that Christ, our God, came to show us."[21]

By 1533, in fact, Las Casas's self-described "long sleep" was over. He once again launched himself into the battleground of justice and liberty for the Amerindians. His first completed book, *The Only Way* was probably finished by 1534 or 1535. In the meantime, Peru was drawing him like a moth to fire, attracted by what apparently was the epicenter of the conquest of Americas in the highlands of South America.[22]

Late in 1534, Las Casas embarked from Santo Domingo for Panama, bound for Peru, bent on accompanying a small contingent of Dominican friars led by Tomás de Berlanga, the newly appointed Bishop of Panama, to evangelize in the land of the Inca. But Las Casas never reached his destination. From the city of Panama, they plunged into the Pacific Ocean but were driven back by largely adverse currents, contrary winds, and maddening calms. The perils of the sea drove them back to the Bay of Panama after weeks of frustration, and from there they transferred to a small coasting vessel bound for Nicaragua, which they reached about the middle of April, 1535.

Nicaragua overwhelmed Las Casas with its beauty, its fertility, its volcanoes, and its gentle people. "This land of Nicaragua," Las Casas wrote from Granada [Nicaragua] in October, 1535, "is the heart and soul of all the Indies, and I judge the Indies to be the most opulent in the whole world."

"Nicaragua is the Lord's paradise," he gushed. "It is the delight and joy for humans. I have seen Española and other islands and parts of Tierra Firme, but none compare with Nicaragua for its fertility, so much

Figure 4.1   Clemente Guido and statue to Indians resisting oppression, Old Leon, Nicaragua, July, 2004. Note Spanish war dog with jaws on the Indian's ankle.

abundance, so pleasant and fresh, so healthy, so many trees, ordered like the orchards of Castile, and finally, everything for man to enjoy life."[23]

He was in Nicaragua for at least a year, until 1536, when he left for Guatemala and Mexico to the north. More exactly, he was expelled from Nicaragua by the Governor and his wife. That the "protector of Indians" began to criticize Spanish rulers and settlers for tormenting Indians soon after his arrival in Nicaragua was almost a given.

Very soon after he arrived in Nicaragua, Las Casas identified the problem. Where are the Indians? The answer was that they were being enslaved and exported to Panama and Peru in a thriving business led by Governor Rodrigo de Contreras (1502–1558) and his wife María de Peñalosa, the daughter of Pedro Arias de Ávila (1440–1531), better known as Pedrarias, and the second governor of Nicaragua. Maria was reputed to be one of the—if not the—richest women in the New World. The Contreras gang—father, wife, and sons who eventually took over the mantle of leadership after the father died—were formidable adversaries. They even murdered their own bishop, Antonio de Valdivieso, in early 1550. Valdivieso, like Las Casas, was a Dominican reformer, actually recommended for his See by Las Casas himself in 1544. That he was martyred—stabbed to death in his own home—gives some insight into this murderous clan.

The Contreras family was running Nicaragua like a private fiefdom when fate washed up Bartolomé de las Casas, protector of American Indians, on their shores. The news of his arrival was greeted with derision and instant suspicion. Why had (mis)fortune delivered this pariah into their little kingdom of Nicaragua? The Contreras were a law unto themselves in Nicaragua, and Las Casas was quick to point this out.

"Open your eyes in the Royal Council [of the Indies] and for God's sake see that in this place the King is neither feared nor obeyed. And like Turks, they don't even pretend to serve the King."[24]

"Do you doubt this?" Las Casas then asked his—perhaps incredulous—correspondent. "Look and know that worse things are said about these governors than even the devils in hell!" Las Casas added a Scriptural passage to support his argument:

When the righteous thrive, the people rejoice;
when the wicked rule, the people groan.
(Prov. 29:2, New International Version)

The people of Nicaragua—the true "wealth" of the province—were being systematically decimated by the governors and settlers. And the conversion of the Indians was but a joke in Nicaragua. As usual, Las

Casas offered solutions. First of all, the enslavement of Indians had to be forbidden. The consequences of the slave trade in Nicaragua were catastrophic.

Las Casas claimed that in the last two years [or 1533–1535] more than twelve thousand souls had been exported to Peru, and they all had died, none had escaped. He continued, saying "They have taken more than twenty-five thousand souls as slaves from here to Panama, and they are all dead. There is not a ship sailing from this port with less than three hundred souls, and they all die of hunger and thirst before reaching Peru."

"They are all dead." It reads like a ghoulish refrain. "And they are all dead."

Of course, they were not all dead, although one can only guess at the mortality rate. Las Casas's penchant for exaggerating has often been the bane of his defenders. The trade in Indians to Panama and Peru could not have been that catastrophic. Otherwise it would have failed altogether. How does one profit from a shipload of starved and dying souls? Even the gruesome Atlantic slave trade probably only had a mortality rate of 10–15 percent over its long course. What good was dead cargo?

Las Casas's unceasing rant against the Contreras provoked them to respond in kind. The Governor's wife knew how to shut him up. She ordered that Las Casas "be pulled down from the pulpit." It was obvious that these people meant business. Pedrarias earlier had had a number of prominent conquistadors executed because they opposed his will. His daughter and son-in-law, the Contreras, were no different.

But Las Casas also meant business. He could do no more here against these barbaric rulers who operated as a law unto themselves. Las Casas shook the dust off his sandals and departed Nicaragua for Guatemala and Mexico. Before leaving he stripped the holy pictures and sacred objects from the monastery where he had been living with his small band of brothers, as if to leave nothing sacred behind to be profaned by these heretics and apostates.

For the next four years, between 1536 and 1540, Las Casas traveled between Guatemala and Mexico, returning to Spain in 1540. As usual, he picked up friends and made enemies as he traveled and preached, pushing his agenda with passion and hot rhetoric. His reputation by now preceded him. In Mexico City, he was welcomed by many of his fellow

Dominicans and Franciscans, some of whom occupied high offices, and he participated in ecclesiastical councils called by the viceroy to decide on issues of Indian slavery, just war, and evangelization. In Guatemala, he persuaded the reformist governor to award him the rights to evangelize a section of the country—Verapaz—that had fiercely, and successfully, resisted the Spanish conquest to now. He preached fiery sermons from the pulpit in Guatemala which prompted equally fiery accusations by settlers and *encomenderos* of pride, arrogance, and ignorance on the part of this priest with the strident voice and condemnatory accusations. In 1540, the Dominicans in Mexico decided to send Las Casas back to Spain to further their causes before the court. He sailed for Spain on the returning fleet of 1540.

The *carrera*, or fleet, was at the heart of the system organized by the Spanish to maintain contact with the expanding American empire. The *carrera* sailed annually from Seville to the colonies. This fleet divided upon reaching the Caribbean and part of it sailed to Panama to service the Viceroyalty of Peru, and the other sailed north to the Viceroyalty of New Spain. The returning fleets, one from Panama and one from Veracruz, then rendezvoused in Havana, Cuba. Loaded down with the silver and other products from the colonies, they sailed from there to Spain, this time as a well-armed fleet called the *Armada de las Indias*. In 1540, the small returning fleet with Las Casas on board departed the Mexican port of Veracruz for Havana in late summer or early fall.

They sailed out of Veracruz on the tide and made the port of call in Havana before heading out into the Atlantic through the Straits of Florida on their way to Spain. Las Casas was in Seville by December, 1540. A new chapter was opening for him.

5

The New Laws of 1542 and Bishop of Chiapa

O n November 20, 1542, in the city of Barcelona, the Emperor Charles V signed into law a decree for the governance of the Indies. The "New Laws of 1542" legislated on the treatment of Indians and replaced the "old" laws issued in the cities of Burgos and Valladolid in 1512 and 1513. The New Laws of 1542 were milestones in Spain's attempt to reform and control the devastating consequences of the conquest in the Americas.

Yet, they were more than the decrees of a monarch, Charles V, bent on bringing unruly and independent-minded *encomenderos* and conquistadors (largely synonymous in this era in many cases) to heel. The laws represented the practical application of newly emerging theories on the nature of man, of freedom, of rights, and even of international law. As such, they stand as monuments to man's spirit and desire to do what is right, on the basis of both Scripture and natural law.

That Las Casas is more closely associated with the laws than anyone else makes them central in his life. They were, in fact, the highlight of his long career. The New Laws, along with his authorship of the *Brief History of the Destruction of the Indies*, which gave fuel to the Black Legend, are, indeed, what he is best known for in the history of Western civilization.

Bartolomé de las Casas and the Conquest of the Americas. Lawrence A. Clayton
© 2011 Lawrence A. Clayton

Laying the groundwork

In 1540, Las Casas returned to Spain after a 20-year absence to recruit more friars for the province of Verapaz in Guatemala. But his goals were considerably more ambitious. For Las Casas, the stage was not merely Guatemala, but it was the fate of Amerindians all across the empire. As he moved around Spain, he continued to write at his usual frenetic pace. He added to his *Brief History of the Destruction of the Indies*, and all the while continued to work on his massive *History of the Indies* from which he extracted much of his other works.

Las Casas lobbied hard with Cardinal García de Loaysa and the Council of the Indies—the governing body for the colonies—to reform the laws governing the Indies. These insistent calls for reform finally prompted Charles in early 1542 to call a special council to convene in Valladolid to study the problems and issue new laws that responded to the criticisms. The agenda of the Indies was once again before the forum of power in Europe. Charles of course knew Las Casas from his youth when he had first come to Spain in 1518. Now the "protector of American Indians" was once again making his case, and Las Casas was a persuasive advocate. He was at his best in 1541–1542.

Other pro-Amerindianists in Spain were as prominent, if not more so, as the energetic Las Casas. One of the leading scholars in Spain, holding a chair at the University of Salamanca, was another Dominican, Francisco de Vitoria (1480–1546). His series of lectures devoted to the nature of the Spanish presence in the Indies, *De Indis*, was published by his students in 1539. It was remarkably similar to the positions held by Las Casas on the claims of Spain to the Indies and there is a definite confluence in the points of view of both Dominicans.

They shared the view, for example, that the "barbarian" nature of the Indians, or their standing outside of Christendom, could not justify making war on them to forcibly accept Christianity. Spaniards and Christians did not have the right by virtue of discovery, conquest, superiority of arms, or any other excuse to strip Amerindians of their rights, their property, their liberty, or their very lives. The only reason for Spaniards to be in the Indies, so Las Casas contended, often with ferocity, was to evangelize. Vitoria generally accepted that position, although he was more politic, and proposed a number of reasons in *De Indis* why the Spanish could legitimately claim sovereignty in the Americas. This included the legitimate right of peoples to trade and engage in commerce with each other, which, in fact, became, in a much more expanded and sophisticated fashion, the basis for the evolution of modern international law.

Vitoria was a sharp, clear-headed, brilliant scholar. But what Las Casas brought to the table was the conviction born of first-hand experience. For Vitoria, the conquistadors and Indians were all pawns in a great chess game, an intellectual construct, although admittedly with immensely important moral and theological significance. What is important to recognize is that Vitoria's *De Indis*, as well as the Papal Bull—*Sublimis Deus*—of 1537, and the writings and actions of other churchmen and scholars contemporaneous with Las Casas, often reflected and confirmed his thinking.

Armed with his own ammunition, and supported by such powerful voices as those of Francisco de Vitoria and Pope Paul III, Las Casas made his arguments day in and day out through the winter and spring of 1542 before the special council in Valladolid. Las Casas's *modus operandi* was to overwhelm his hearers with evidence in almost numbing detail.

> Las Casas's technique in achieving these goals was powerful and dramatic …
> For hours without interruption he held the councilors motionless with a complete reading of the *Decimation* (the memorial on atrocities), while his two aides, the friar and the Indian, displayed piles of notarized proofs to back what he was describing.[1]

The *Decimation* was Las Casas's draft of *A Brief History of the Destruction of the Indies*, which he later published in 1552.

Las Casas's hearers sat on for hour after hour, week after week, as the story of brutality, greed, and injustice almost overwhelmed their senses. Las Casas read for days on end. The counselors listened, not simply because they had been ordered to do so by the Emperor, but also because the account rendered by Las Casas was absolutely compelling. It was not just Las Casas's rendition; it was the testimony of witnesses who could not be ignored by even the most calloused and jaded counselors. Charles attended some of the sessions and, when absent, received a summary of each day's proceedings from his own confidants.

Las Casas named names as he laid out his history of the conquest: Pedrarias de Ávila, Nuño de Guzmán, Pedro de Alvarado, Francisco Pizarro (the worst of the lot in Las Casas's opinion), and even Hernán Cortés did not escape the list. What adds power to the narrative was the near constant refrain, and "*y yo lo ví*" from his lips: "And I saw these things." Las Casas did not carry the weight of the Pope or the intellectual influence of a Francisco de Vitoria, nor was he as elegant and persuasive in Latin as some of his peers. But he brought the power of the eyewitness to the bar of justice, and justice was what he demanded as he read from *The Brief History*.

Never at a loss for solutions, Las Casas also read from his *Sixteen Remedies*, of which the most important was the Eighth Remedy. This one suggested putting all the Indians under the immediate authority of the Crown and abolishing the *encomienda*. He laid out his arguments carefully: the evangelization of the Indians was the only possible reason for Spaniards to be in the New World and the greatest obstacle to this overriding goal was the *encomienda*. At stake were not only the souls of the natives, but of Spaniards and of the very Emperor as well; everything the Indians have been deprived of—their liberty, property, lives, dominion—should be restored—the principle of restitution.

"The *encomienda*," Las Casas spoke directly, "is a wild root which contaminates the entire plant's branches, flowers, and fruit."[2]

Passion "shot out of Las Casas's eyes and mouth," recalled one observer.[3] "He would downright sputter" when on the subject of the *encomenderos*. The effect on his hearers was dramatic. If predisposed to be sympathetic, they were won over. If antagonistic to the defender of the Indians, their suspicion and antagonism usually turned to hatred, for Las Casas divided rather than united. He alternated between excoriating the conquistadors and *encomenderos* in language reminiscent of Old Testament prophets like Isaiah and Jeremiah, and then spoke of the sheep in the tender, almost loving, words of the pastor, like the apostle Paul of the New Testament. It was a side of the defender of Indians not seen too often, moved by the qualities of mercy, charity, and gentleness.

"Your Excellencies, we received a new calling from the Lord," Las Casas spoke during one session. "Our new calling was to give the faith to these simple and innocent infidels, held in the bosom of the father of families, our God, so that in the hour of judgment of this world, they may receive the promise of eternal life. Through the vine of our Church's eternal life they should be called sweetly and with praise, not dragged in by the yoke of infernal servitude which they have suffered, and are suffering."[4]

"The faith has been sold to them at great cost, too great a cost, Excellencies," Las Casas continued. "Christ taught us that freely it has been given to us, and freely we are to give to others."

Most of the council members knew Scripture well enough, especially the churchmen in the group. Las Casas challenged them to judge from the high bar of Christian virtue, and be obedient to Scripture, reminding them repeatedly of their calling. But he also opened the window into the pit of hell created by the sins of the conquest. It was a double-barreled approach that drove home his arguments.

To undo the evil perpetuated in the conquest of the Indies Las Casas made specific with regard to what was required of Charles: end the *encomienda*, restore freedom to those forced into bondage or slavery, acknowledge the right of Indians to be sovereign in their own lands, and accept the proposition that the conquest was in fact illegal, immoral, and reversible.

Charles, of course operated, in a larger world context than Las Casas, whose single issue drove him with a passion. Charles had to consider the Empire. So, while he pondered restoring Peru to the Incas (restitution), he probably considered it only in theory as he listened to the impassioned Las Casas.

Charles listened as closely to Francisco de Vitoria as to Las Casas on this issue. Vitoria argued persuasively that a complete withdrawal from the Indies would undermine the very reason (the only reason Las Casas and his supporters argued) for the Spaniards to be in the Indies: to evangelize and spread Christianity. Without being there, no matter how debatable the controversial circumstances, how could evangelization, which all agreed was positive, take place?[5]

If Peru, and the rest of the Indies, were abandoned because of Las Casas's crazed opinion, driven—many of his critics accused—by the "Prince of Darkness" who was using Las Casas as his tool, then "the light of the gospel" in the Indies would be snuffed out. What is certain is that Charles certainly considered in theory the most radical of Las Casas's proposals for remedying the ills of the Indies, and these included abandonment and restitution. The stage was set for the final redaction of the New Laws.

When approved and signed by Charles on November 20, 1542, in Barcelona, the New Laws produced shock waves across the Indies. Peruvian conquistadors rebelled against the Crown, and Las Casas was at the center of this firestorm of protest and rebellion as the "author" of the New Laws. They hated the defender of Indians for not only inspiring the New Laws, but also for nailing them to the cross of guilt and sin.

At the heart of the New Laws was the suppression of Indian slavery and the provision to end the *encomienda* after the lifetime of the present holders. The New Laws provided not only for sweeping reforms in the relationship between settlers and Indians, but also for new administrative initiatives and reforms.

Five basic principles and actions were clearly articulated:

- the dignity of the Indian as subjects of the Crown;
- the elimination of Indian slavery;
- provisions for the extinction of the *encomienda* as a principal form of exploiting the Indian as labor and vassal;
- prohibiting wars of conquest;
- strict and detailed laws and decrees for the enforcement of all the above.

All *encomiendas* held by royal and ecclesiastical officials were immediately revoked and the Indians placed under the authority of royal officials in the Indies. Never short of details, Las Casas-inspired specifics breathed life into the new statutes. In Peru, for example, certain people involved in a recent rebellion were stripped of their Indians immediately. In New Spain, nine *encomiendas* with excessive numbers of Indians were reduced to a moderate size. And then the bombshell: No new *encomiendas* were to be created and all existing private *encomiendas* would revert to the Crown upon the death of the present holder. It was, in fact, the death knell of the *encomienda* system, or so thought Las Casas and his supporters.

The Crown, of course, stood to benefit as well, diverting the labor and usufruct derived from the *encomiendas* immediately in some instances,

Figure 5.1 The cover of the famous New Laws of 1542 that propelled Las Casas to the forefront of the battle for control of the Amerindians. These laws were received in the Indies with vituperation and hatred for Las Casas, who was considered their spiritual author.

and eventually in others, into Crown coffers. Furthermore, the power of the *encomendero*/conquistador class would be seriously undermined by the New Laws, furthering the centralization of power in the monarchy and reducing the potential for rebellious Spaniards in the Indies to throw off allegiance to the monarchy.

And one other trend was already far advanced, and quite evident to all: the increasingly dramatic drop in Amerindian population across the Indies. As the Amerindians died off, so did the value of the *encomiendas*, and settlers were already consciously seeking other forms of income, such as acquiring landed estates (*haciendas*), in mining, and in commerce. The *encomienda* as the backbone of wealth was giving way to other forms of wealth acquisition and making a living. But in 1542, they still symbolized the power acquired by the conquistador class through their own arms and efforts and they fiercely resisted an encroachment on these rights. Not only did the New Laws restrict the *encomiendas*, but, additionally, any further *entradas*, or expeditions of discovery, conquest, and settlement, were proscribed by the New Laws.

In 1573, King Philip II, Charles's son who succeeded to the throne in 1556, confirmed and expanded these instructions for new conquests with even greater restrictions. The era of unbridled and unabashed expansion that had brought Spain and her warriors into control of much of the Americas was coming to an end.

However, as far as Las Casas was concerned, the New Laws were a good start but did not go far enough in uprooting the evil. He returned to Valladolid with his old friend and traveling companion, Rodrigo de Andrada, and drafted a memorial of needed emendations. These tended to make them truly "draconian," in keeping with Las Casas's compulsive character.[6]

"Fray Bartolomé de las Casas and fray Rodrigo de Andrada," the memorial opens, "say that Your Majesty *has commenced* [italics added] to … ," and it continues its prologue extolling the great work of light and liberty which the Emperor had launched, but the work had only commenced.[7] This long memorial requested tightening the New Laws to reflect Las Casas's deep suspicions that the laws would be evaded or circumvented. In the end, Prince Philip, who governed Spain for much of 1543 in the absence of his father, issued a revised set of laws in June, 1543, which clarified the New Laws, incorporating some of what Las Casas had offered as amendments.

When the specifics of the New Laws reached the Indies, they shocked the conquistador-*encomendero* class. The crazed cleric was once more on the assault, and they were squarely in the crosshairs of his sights. In Peru, an outright rebellion greeted the New Laws. In New Spain, the special representative of the Crown, Francisco Tello de Sandoval, sent to implement the New Laws, instead suspended their publication until further notice; otherwise he too faced rebellion. In Guatemala, the entire blame for the New Laws was laid on Las Casas. The defender of American Indians was excoriated as a scandalous, vain-glorious, ignorant prelate. The leading citizens of Guatemala noted that Las Casas had spent most of his years in Cuba and La Española, precisely where the greatest losses of Indian life had occurred, and Las Casas was responsible in part for the very acts he condemned. And, as for his expertise on Guatemala, "in this land," they wrote to the Emperor, "he just passed through on his way to Mexico, and since he didn't find support there [Mexico] for his scandalous accusations, he returned to us, as if we were fools."[8]

As for Las Casas, he was not satisfied with the New Laws, even with the amendments. But it was a beginning. The hand of providence, from the perspective of his supporters, was about to move again in his life, although his detractors no doubt viewed Satan once more intervening. In 1543, Las Casas was offered a bishopric in the Indies. He took it and returned to the New World, this time with a bishop's mitre and authority to enforce good.

Bishop of Chiapa

In 1543, he accepted the bishopric of Chiapa, which included territories in northern Guatemala and southern Mexico. Las Casas was drawn passionately to the region, and he wanted to bring his Verapaz experiment to fruition and success, and Verapaz was part of the territory of his new See. Basically the experiment was premised on excluding secular Spaniards from the region, allowing only priests and friars into the region.

The dual roles of thinker and activist were inexorably linked in his persona, but at times in his life, like now, he pursued one with greater passion than the other. Furthermore, he never forgot why he had returned to Spain in 1540: to recruit more resources and soldiers of the

Cross for his activities in Guatemala and Verapaz, and to return with a company of Dominican friars-recruits to support those he had left behind.

He was consecrated Bishop on March 30, 1544, in his hometown of Seville. While he was busy with preparations for his return to Chiapa, a warm reception was also being planned in the Indies by those whose interests were most affected by the laws. Upon hearing of Las Casas's imminent return, the Cabildo, or municipal council, of Santiago de Guatemala wrote the King in September, 1543 that "we are as disturbed as if [the public executioner] had been sent to cut off our heads."⁹

"This friar [Las Casas]," they wrote, was "not learned, not saintly, but envious, vainglorious, passionate, restless, and touched with greed," attributes—especially the latter—usually hurled by Las Casas at the *encomendero* and settler class in the Indies. "The father deceives himself," the Cabildo's letter continued, "may God forgive him. There are others who know just as much and somewhat more than he, who have reflected on and studied the problem with holy zeal and without passion, and who seek nothing more than Your Majesty's welfare and that of these poor people."¹⁰

In the meantime, Francisco Tello de Sandoval had suspended the publication of the New Laws in New Spain, while many churchmen, among them the provincials of the Dominicans, Franciscans, and Augustinians in New Spain, joined the chorus of colonists in demanding the retraction of these laws that were depicted as the ruin of the colonies. Although hardly oblivious to the chorus of denunciations echoing across the Indies, Las Casas moved imperturbably on his appointment as the new Bishop of Chiapa.

What was Las Casas's full agenda as Bishop? That it was considerably more than being a shepherd to his flock is a given. But how ambitious was he? Las Casas wanted to create a model bishopric where Indians were protected and given preference, and secular (avaricious, greedy) Spaniards were either kept at a distance or were banished by a rigorous application of the New Laws. To do this he needed funds, laborers, and a large extension of territory that included as many Indians as possible. Las Casas's vision was, as usual, expansive and ambitious. And now with a Bishop's authority, he was also freed somewhat from strict obedience to his own order, the Dominicans. He remained, of course, a friar and a Dominican, but he added the authority of the Bishop's mitre to his resources.

He received from the Pope and Prince Philip—continuing to act as Regent of Spain in his father's absence—additions of territory to his bishopric. The provinces of Tuzulutlán and Lancandón were recognized by a royal decree of February 13, 1544, as part of his See. Soconusco on the Pacific coast was added, and most of modern Yucatán as well, which did not receive its own bishopric until 1561.

As he traveled across Spain in 1543–1544, he recruited almost fifty Dominicans and a few lay people. In early January, 1544, they began their travels from Valladolid and Salamanca to Seville, where they eventually embarked for the New World. One of them, fray Tomás de la Torre, was commissioned by his superior to keep a record of the trip.

He recorded the full trip faithfully, from the freezing heartland of Spain to the tropical coast of New Spain. There is no better story or history of such a trip. The events that marked the trip could not have been invented. They included everything from betrayal, floods, pirates, shipwrecks, misery, courage, treason, and nobility, in the face of adversity at which most of us would quickly buckle. That the odyssey was undertaken as a calling of God, rather than by the lure of gold, wealth, and fame, makes it even more compelling testimony to the devotion of these friars.[11]

After a short stop in San Juan, Puerto Rico, they arrived at Santo Domingo on September 9, 1544, and, accompanied by the roar of cannon fire to celebrate their arrival, they dropped anchor.

The long voyage, aboard the leaky, badly-sailed *San Salvador* anticipated what lay ahead for Las Casas. The man held largely responsible for the New Laws of 1542 was received, along with his retinue of Dominican friar-recruits, as a pariah in the Indies. But like some people who thrive on stress and challenge, Las Casas was not fazed or puzzled. If anything, it hardened his will to prevail. The next three years, or from his arrival in Santo Domingo in September, 1544, until his return to Spain in April, 1547, were the most dramatic in his life, already marked by extraordinary highs and lows.

The procession of his friars into Santo Domingo to the Dominican monastery was a good precursor of what lay ahead. About thirty formed the procession, with Bishop Las Casas following at the rear. The Bishop of Santo Domingo, Rodrigo de Bastidas, received them warmly at the steps of the monastery. On the other hand, "the processional march of his devout young friars, following the example of Sevillian religious brotherhoods, was greeted not with sympathy but with jeers and ridicule."[12]

Las Casas's old nemesis, the conquistador-historian Gonzalo Fernández de Oviedo, was nearby and watched it all. Oviedo was also a veteran soldier and occupied the position of *alcaide*, or captain, of the Santo Domingo fortress. "I saw them come into the city," Oviedo wrote, "two by two, thirty of them in all, chanting, with their tunics and escapularies and hats and their capes, and the bishop bringing up the rear."[13]

Upon reaching the monastery, the prior greeted the new arrivals warmly where they were blessed and prayed together. The new bishop and his company were soon involved in a test of wills that would have rapidly brought an ordinary man to his knees. By now the word had spread throughout the Indies that Las Casas was the author of the hated New Laws. That hatred was easily transposed from the New Laws to its author who had dared to return to the Indies, even as a newly appointed Bishop with the support of the Emperor Charles and his son, Prince Philip. A pox on all three of them was the consensus of the *encomenderos* and Indian slaveholders throughout the land.

The hospitality and love within the monastery, compared to the vituperation and hatred outside, could not have been more pronounced than if the young friars were passing between two entirely different universes. And perhaps they were. Inside the monastery they were welcomed, given the cells of other friars, and the father provincial even served them while dining, washed their feet, and gave them everything he could. Ever solicitous of their health, spiritual and natural, he ordered them all to eat meat and dispensed with fasting days so they could recover their health from such a long and trying sea voyage.

Outside the reception was brutal. Since the laws freeing the slaves had already been published, fray Torre remarked, the Spaniards only viewed the bishop as the devil, for they knew him in that land and they knew that he always had treated and still treated the Indians with great favor. "And since we came with him," Torre continued, "they also showed us ill will and didn't want to give us food and even withheld food from the monastery since we were there."

Everyone, rich and poor, felt the bishop was undermining their liveli-hood: the rich because they were being stripped of their wealth or could not get wealthier, and the poor because they were deprived of the chance to get rich. "And all the rest felt the same way," Antonio de Remesal an early biographer, wrote in the seventeenth century. "The bishop, as far as all concerned, was to blame. No one visited him in the monastery they hated him so much, nor was he welcomed, and they heaped insults on him."[14]

Ever suspicious of his enemies, Las Casas did not trust the laws to be put into effect.[15] How right he was. His intelligence was very accurate. He had already heard that Sandoval had not published the New Laws in New Spain and that twelve spokesmen [*procuradores*; a legal representa-tive sent to represent one's position] had been sent from New Spain to appeal the laws, and that among them were friars. In Las Casas's mind, this was nothing short of treason, heresy. "I appeal to Your Highness, for the love of Jesus Christ, to consider the motives that each one has and how evil and injustice can be hidden and covered." The cold, hateful reception that Las Casas received in Santo Domingo had angered him, and his scorn and condemnation of his enemies poured out in a letter to Prince Philip.

The *encomenderos* and their supporters were bent on destroying a part of humanity, without anyone stopping them, breaking not only man-made laws but also the laws of God.

"I beg Your Highness," Las Casas wrote, knowing his life's work was at stake, "with all the obedience and respect I owe my Prince, and ask you a thousand times, if necessary, to hold them off until I can return to defend the liberty of my sheep."[16] Las Casas desperately wanted to be in Spain, at court, to refute the destroyers of his sheep, but he also had another mission. If it was possible for a man already running at full speed, he redoubled his efforts to get on with the journey to his bishopric which, conveniently, was within the Viceroyalty of New Spain. He wanted to get at his most insistent and powerful critics and he found them in spades whereever he traveled.

The rumor mill was afire in the monastery with the news coming in from across the Indies. In New Spain, the laws had been rejected; in Peru, people who defended the laws were getting murdered. The friars won-dered how they would be received in New Spain, coming, as they were, in the service of the very man who was considered to be the author of the New Laws. "We heard," Torre wrote, "that they have rebelled in Peru and killed the Viceroy [true] and burned all the ships they found in the ports so no one could take news back to Spain," and, Torre added ominously, "they killed one of our friars as well."

"We didn't know what to do, for when we arrive in New Spain they will probably kill the Bishop and us also." This work for God was, as Las Casas had discovered over the years, very dangerous. Amid prayer, studying, and preaching, the friars awaited for the Bishop to finish their travel arrangements.

Soon after they sailed, they hit a storm on December 16 that lasted until near Christmas. The last night of the storm was the worst. The rain beat down on them and Torre recorded that the waves seemed to reach to heaven, and they thought their final hour had arrived for sure. The waves crashed over the poop deck and winds brought down the foremast. "Some of the friars commended themselves to God, others cried out the name of our Lord Jesus Christ, and the old saint [Las Casas] commanded the seas in the name of N. S. J. [Nuestro Señor Jesús; Our Lord Jesus] to be quiet and still and he told the people to be quiet and not to fear, that God was with us and we couldn't perish."[17]

The friars sang hymns and were consoled by the Bishop's call on God to save them. As they sang and sang, a crewman, sensing a change in the seas and wind, told them "Fathers, the storm has stopped." And, "as if an angel had told us, we began to sing a 'Te Deum Laudamus' and a great calm replaced the storm."

Had a miracle occurred? "I'm not a friend," fray Torre later wrote, "of calling something a miracle that can be explained by natural causes, but I told it like it happened. You readers can put your own judgment on it. We gave thanks to God, certain that He saved us in the way that served Him."

They celebrated Christmas at sea with hymns and prayers, a candlelight vigil on Christmas Eve, all complete with an effigy of the baby Jesus in a cradle of hay. On Christmas Day, 1544, they sighted land, and rejoiced. On December 26, Las Casas preached a sermon as they coasted along the Caiman Islands off southwestern Cuba towards the Yucatán peninsula. On January 6, 1545, they reached the port of Campeche, on

Figure 5.2   Father Martin de Ayala instructs Felipe Guaman Poma de Ayala, a native Peruvian Amerindian, and his parents in the Christian faith.

the western shore of Yucatán. They had arrived finally on the mainland of the Viceroyalty of New Spain.

A little fleet of canoes sallied forth from the port to bring Las Casas and his friars to shore. The canoes were filled with Indians and Spaniards, the Indians doing all the paddling of course, almost naked except for loincloths to cover their private parts. The local priest also rode out to the ship to greet the new Bishop. The Indians were curious, animated, excited. The Spaniards seemed sullen and not very friendly. The reception was repeated often in the course of the next two years.

A few Spaniards on the beach kneeled before the Bishop and received his benediction. Bartolomé de las Casas, he might be, the author of the hated New Laws, but he was still a bishop of the Church. Besides, these Spaniards were not the *encomenderos* and rulers of the land and its people. More modest in their pretensions, they saw only their new bishop. By habit and tradition, they deferred to his office.

The Governor of the Province of Yucatán was Francisco de Montejo. The Bishop sent a messenger to the Governor announcing his arrival. This news was probably greeted by Montejo as a doomsday kind of announcement. Las Casas thought little of Montejo, whose father had preceded him in the conquest of Yucatán.

"Your majesty's laws and authority," Las Casas reported back to the emperor, "are no more obeyed in Yucatán any more than if they were from Barbarroxa [Barbarroja, a famous Muslim Algerian warrior, the archenemy of Spanish Christians]." In the meantime, fray Torre and his companions took stock of Campeche and the surrounding countryside, beginning to perceive for themselves the reasons for their Bishop's intensity and devotion to the Indians.

"All the people in this province," Torre recorded, "are infidels and unbaptized since there is no one to teach them anything. The Christians which the King has sent to the Indians to teach them and bring them to an understanding of God don't teach them anything, but instead rob and strip them, killing men, raping women, without thought or scruples. That's the way it was in the beginning, and the way it is now."

Torre's narrative could have been written by the Bishop himself. "Put up a church and an image of a ferocious Spaniard with a cross in one hand and a sword in the other, mounted on horseback, slaying men. They call this an image of Santiago [St. James] and they order all to worship it and there's hardly a town without one. They also nail up a Cross and if it rains, or there's a drought, or a pestilence or some other evil occurs, the Indians say that stick did it and they beg their masters to take it away."

"And the Spaniards don't know what to say," Torre continued, somewhat contemptuously, "other than that the cross is a good thing and the Indians were stupid dogs if they didn't want to believe in God."

The lack of understanding of the true tenets of Christianity was obvious everywhere to Torre and his companions. "The Indians don't believe in the immortality of the soul," he recorded, "and little doctrine is taught or known. Some Indian women were baptized since Spaniards who wished to take them didn't want to violate their scruples and so they have the women baptized."[18]

"The secular Spaniards defended themselves by claiming these things needed to be the way they were so the Spaniards could make a living, but our Lord opened our eyes from the beginning," Torre wrote, "so that we would see, and do something and so avoid the blindness of the rest." Las Casas was well aware of their reactions to the world of injustice around them, and he took care to keep his charges alive to the needs of the Indians as he had seen them now almost all his life.

On the next leg of the trip, by sea from Campeche to Tabasco, nine of his friars tragically died in an accident at sea. Las Casas had put them, as well as other passengers, on an old bark that foundered just off the coast, and the loss dismayed his young followers. Nonetheless, Las Casas and the rest of the friars and retinue pressed on, arriving in Chiapa on February 3, 1545.

The capital of his See had a magnificent name, the Royal City of the Plains of Chiapa, but was quite a bit more humble than its resplendent name. About sixty Spanish householders lived there, with their Indians. It was in the tropics but, at 6,700 feet above sea level, high enough to have a pleasant climate.

But no one felt pleasant or amiable when the Bishop and his friars arrived. The settlers had been incited by letters from across the Indies, such as one which read: "We say here that the sins of your land must be very great indeed, when God punishes it with such an affliction as sending that anti-Christ for bishop!"[19]

It did not take the Bishop long to issue a proclamation to the faithful on March 20, 1545. It was an edict directed at public sins committed by both laity and clergy, and called on all to denounce and reveal where and when and who might be in sin. It was not unusual for a Bishop to initiate his duties in a new See this way. It was his responsibility to make an annual examination of the life and habits of all his subjects, both clerical and secular in accordance with his conscience for the welfare and health of their souls, and the Bishop called on all who knew of public vices and sins to come forth and denounce the sinners.[20] However, Las Casas's edit was particularly scathing and hostile, almost "inquisitorial in its fiery tone." The Bishop was, in effect, firing the first shot across the bow of his parishioners.

That virtually all of the Spanish settlers and *encomenderos* were in sin was a given for Las Casas. Indian slavery was common throughout the region of Guatemala, Yucatán, and Chiapa, and the slave trade was carried out openly—and brazenly—in the very heart of Chiapa.

The scene was set for a titanic battle, and it was not long in coming. It, in fact, mirrored what was occurring across the Indies, for the New Laws had provoked not only resentment but also outright rebellion on the part of the *encomendero* class and their supporters. "The reaction took various forms ... town meetings, tolling bells, riots, outright revolts."[21] In Peru, the first viceroy, Blasco Núñez Vela, was captured and beheaded by Francisco Pizarro's brother, Gonzalo. The symbolism and act of executing the Emperor's emissary could hardly have been plainer. Royal officials across the Indies backed away from the New Laws, suspending or simply refusing to enforce the more onerous ones, such as the one outlawing Indian slavery and another disinheriting the *encomenderos*. In the face of this general enmity, the Bishop of Chiapa flung the gauntlet down at his slave-holding parishioners. They flung it back in his face, with swords drawn at the bold Bishop who threatened their very livelihood in this life, and their souls in the next.

The citizens, however, initially received their new Bishop with a welcome—though cool—appropriate to his station. Upon reaching Chiapa, even the Cabildo welcomed him formally, although only one *regidor* and one *alcalde* were present, the rest absent for obvious, and perhaps ominous, reasons.[22] So, a welcome was extended, but not a friendly one. Perhaps the Bishop could be persuaded to modify his historic and well-known intransigence.

That was wishful thinking. Las Casas chose the sacrament of confession as his weapon of choice. Only four priests were permitted by Las Casas to hear confessions, and the Bishop reserved the right to hear confessions and absolve sins in special cases, which included slave-holding and trafficking in slaves. Easter was approaching when the faithful were obliged to go to confession and receive absolution in order to take communion and it was a perfect occasion for "episcopal correction."[23]

The Bishop dropped the axe on Easter Sunday when he took the pulpit. He struck at the slaveholders first. They were forbidden to confess and receive absolution for their sins unless they first freed all slaves illegally obtained, and made proper restitution. In the Bishop's mind, all Indian slavery was forbidden. Everyone guilty of extortionate and inhumane practices had to obey the Bishop. Otherwise, there would be no confession, no absolution and, ultimately, excommunication.

The townspeople roared in defiance, appealing to the Bishop to come to his senses. Slave owners had always been confessed and absolved. No Indians, they claimed, would obey a Spaniard if the slave trade ceased and the losses from releasing slaves would be tremendous. Papal bulls were dragged out to justify war and slavery, while other high-ranking critics threatened to go straight to the Council of the Indies, the Emperor and the Pope. Las Casas was thoroughly damned, condemned as a friend of Indian dogs and no friend of true Christians. Some slave owners, desperate to confess and be absolved, promised to liberate their slaves on certain conditions, hoping the Bishop would relent. One, for example, said he was in the middle of building his home, and once he was finished in four months, the slaves would be freed. Others made similar promises, but Las Casas was unrelenting. He read them the New Laws verbatim.

"We've heard them, father," they responded.

"Well, then, obey them," was the Bishop's retort and command.

"We've appealed them." So had others across the colonies. Later that fall, on October 20, 1545, the Emperor, faced with open rebellion in Peru and persuaded by a generous bribe from the colonists, revoked some of the most obnoxious ordinances, including the one limiting *encomiendas* to one or two lifetimes. But that was later. This was now.

A campaign of slander called the Bishop a fool, a glutton, not even an "old" Christian, implying his ancestors were Jewish or Muslim converts. One night one partisan, moved by the increasingly strident cacophony, fired off a harquebus with a blast outside the Bishop's residence, probably pleased with himself and congratulated by his cronies for striking terror into the Bishop's heart. The fools were, however, on the streets, not in the house. The townspeople were in a near riot, demanding retractions from the Bishop, clamoring before him, waving the Papal Donation of 1493 to justify war and enslavement, buzzing loudly that this bishop, "a disturber of the peace ... a foe of Christians and a protector of Indian dogs" must go. Even the dean of the cathedral, Gil Quintana, openly disobeyed the Bishop's orders.

On the day after Easter, Father Gil Quintana heard the confession of three or four notorious slaveholders. Las Casas summoned this disobedient priest to explain himself. Quintana refused. After the fifth summons, and fifth refusal, the Bishop sent his bailiff to arrest the obstinate, not to speak of insubordinate, Quintana. The dean of the cathedral drew his sword to protect himself. Not much of a swordsman, he stabbed himself in the hand and the Bishop's bailiff nicked his leg. As the dean was escorted out of his house, a huge, angry crowd gathered. Quintana struggled with the bailiff.

"Help me, sirs!" Quintana pleaded to the crowd. "I'll confess you all," he shouted, then, thinking quickly, he added "get me loose, and I'll absolve you too!"

"Whereupon," one biographer, Henry Wagner, laconically observed, "a full-scale riot erupted." The crowd shoved the bailiff aside and freed Quintana, surging toward the bishop's house, which they stormed, brandishing weapons, shouting, as they entered. Standing in the middle of the room was the Bishop, facing them down with disdain. Some of Las Casas's visitors quickly drew their swords and stepped in front to protect the Bishop. He tried to wave them aside. He needed no one but God, but his friends thought a swordsman or two might not contradict God's will.

"I'll kill the traitor!" shouted the man who earlier had fired the harquebus. He waved his short sword and made for Las Casas. But cooler heads prevailed. A couple of townspeople restrained the man and someone nodded towards the door. The swaggering, shouting knot of bullies a moment earlier now slinked out, still murmuring but subdued. This particular battle was over, but the war for the Indians between Las Casas and the great mass of conquistadors, officials, and early settlers continued.

For the next two years, or until the middle of 1547, when the Bishop returned to Spain, Las Casas sparred with his enemies in Verapaz, Guatemala, and Mexico. He threatened to excommunicate the Viceroy and all the judges of the Audiencia of Mexico. He drew up a list of requirements to be met before confession could be given to *encomenderos* and Indian slaveholders. If obeyed, these ordinances would have stripped them of authority and power over Indian subjects. In short, he went about his business with characteristic disdain for his personal safety and totally committed to relieving the afflictions of the Indians.

But, faced with rebellion, the New Laws were gutted of their most controversial provisions by the Emperor's retractions, and Las Casas decided once again to return to Spain. In April, 1547, he embarked for the transatlantic crossing at the port of Veracruz, and once in Spain, never returned to the Indies. In 1550, he became immersed in the most fascinating debate in the history of sixteenth-century Europe, a milestone in the history of human rights.

6

"All Mankind is One"

On the Nature of Humans, Servitude, and Slavery

The return voyage, from April to June, 1547, was pleasant. Las Casas was at another of those major junctures in his life. He had come home with the intention of resigning his bishopric of Chiapa, itself an admission of failure. But he did not yield to any sense of defeat. If anything, the intransigence of the settlers and *encomenderos* in the Indies stiffened his resolve to continue in his trajectory as universal protector of Indians.

His rules for confession and absolution had produced havoc in Chiapa. Some *encomenderos*, refusing to acknowledge the rules, "died pleading in vain for the last rites of the Church" wrote Lewis Hanke.[1] Other *encomenderos* retaliated with a tried and true tactic: withhold alms and tithes from the Dominicans, starve the friars into submission. Some settlers even threatened violence against Las Casas's companions attempting to follow his rules for confessors.

Emboldened by the suspension of the most detested of the New Laws, *encomenderos* throughout the Indies campaigned to make the *encomiendas* perpetual, handed down from father to son forever. This was like waving a red flag before the Bishop of Chiapa. An enemy of the *encomienda* ever since he renounced his own on the island of Cuba in 1514, the idea of making it perpetual drove him to a fury, and he fought this new challenge for the rest of his life.

The battle waged between the detractors and defenders of Amerindians in Spain took place until mid-century, largely on the stage set by the

Bartolomé de las Casas and the Conquest of the Americas. Lawrence A. Clayton
© 2011 Lawrence A. Clayton

meetings of the Council of the Indies. When Las Casas argued before the Council, he poured out petitions, memorials, and scandalous tales of woe and disaster. He seemed to have a bottomless supply of them, and he continued to write at a frantic pace between 1547 and 1552, when he published many of his tracts and polemics.

The debates before the Council in 1550 highlighted the divisive issues raised by Las Casas. Appearing for the *encomenderos* on numerous occasions was, for example, Bernal Díaz de Castillo, a veteran of Cortés's campaigns in the conquest of Mexico, and himself an *encomendero*. In a few years he composed one of the most colorful narratives of the conquest of Mexico, but at this juncture he was promoting the interests of the *encomenderos* of both the Viceroyalties of Peru and New Spain.

At first, the Council generally accepted Díaz de Castillo's arguments made in 1550: the Indians are better treated and instructed in the Holy Faith by the *encomenderos*; the service of God and the protection of the Royal Patrimony (the King's pocketbook) are best served by the *encomienda*; the royal conscience is important to the *encomenderos*, whose virtuous acts will preserve it (the conscience) intact.

Then Las Casas and his small but powerful cohort of friends responded before the Council. They tore into Díaz de Castillo's arguments, and the Council was persuaded to postpone any recommendation to the Crown on the possible perpetuity of the *encomienda* until Charles, again away from Spain, returned. Díaz de Castillo returned to Guatemala disgusted. "Such an excellent thing," he later wrote, "never was accomplished, and in this manner we proceed, like a lame mule, from bad to worse, and from one Viceroy to another and from Governor to Governor."[2]

By 1550, Las Casas had persuaded the Emperor to instruct the Council of the Indies to convene a special committee of theologians and jurists to sit in judgment on the specific issue: "Is it lawful for the King of Spain to wage war on the Indians, before preaching the faith to them, in order to subject them to his rule, so that afterward they may be more easily instructed in the faith?"[3]

The *encomenderos* and their defenders had recently recruited the most renowned Aristotelian scholar in all of Spain, Juan Ginés de Sepúlveda, to draw up an indictment of the Indian nature. Sepúlveda and Las Casas faced each other in a debate in 1550 before this special council convened by Charles. This council was to determine the larger truths of the matter:

was the conquest legal; and were the Indians themselves denied their basic rights as human beings?

Sepúlveda's basic premise was drawn from his interpretation of Aristotle's taxonomy of humankind that divided men into two groups, those born to rule, and those born to be ruled. Las Casas had been insisting before Charles, Philip, and the Council of the Indies that the conquests be halted and all Indians be freed and put under the authority of the Crown as originally intended by the New Laws of 1542. This, of course, would strip the *encomenderos* of their power and livelihood. Even though pulled by other pressing matters of church and state, Charles listened as the debate proceeded.

Charles was a complicated ruler, part medieval, part Machiavellian, imbued with a deep Christian faith and chivalric values. Las Casas must have sounded at times like a hysterical Old Testament-style prophet to Charles, but prophets were not ordinary people, given to ordinary admonitions.

Who was right in all this? Las Casas? Sepúlveda? In the minds of Catholics of the times, true freedom (from sin) came only by repentance and forgiveness, and through the redemptive work of Christ on the cross.[4] Could one expect forgiveness if the blood of Indians was on the record against you? With some of the above in mind, Charles convened the special council and suspended all conquests (April 16, 1550) until the council heard the debate and came to a decision.

Juan Ginés de Sepúlveda enjoyed a high scholarly reputation. He had translated two of Aristotle's works, had been educated at the universities of Alcalá de Henares in Spain and Bologna in Italy, and had served as an assistant to Cardinal Tomás de Vio Cayetano (1469–1534) in the preparation of the New Testament in Spanish. His sharp intellect pushed him to the forefront of Counter-Reformation forces in Spain, especially in refuting the teachings of Martin Luther. In 1535, he was named chaplain of the Emperor Charles.

Sometime in 1546 or 1547, Sepúlveda was approached by Cardinal Loaysa, then President of the Council of the Indies and no friend of Las Casas and the Indianists, and asked for a learned opinion upholding the just causes of war against the Indians. This treatise, not very long and written in a few days, was given the title of *Democrates alter, sive de justis belli causus apud Indos.* The work is sometime known as *Democrates segunda* since its arguments closely parallel an earlier work he wrote in 1535, *Democrates primus.*

Las Casas's anger erupted when he returned to Spain and read Sepúlveda's treatise, whose principal premise was that "wars against the Indians were just, and even constituted a necessary preliminary to their Christianization."[5] Sepúlveda argued that just wars allowed for the enslavement of the vanquished by the victors and all that implied. The Indians were obviously "inferior" to the Spaniards, in the same fashion that children were to adults, women to men, indeed, almost like apes to men. These Indians could not be "reduced" to the Christian faith by evangelization alone, of which there are many cases of tragic failure. Missionaries had been slaughtered in Venezuela and New Spain and the Indians reverted to their barbaric ways once soldiers were withdrawn. Force could be employed to convert them, as Scripture was interpreted by Saint Augustine. Some contended that wars could not be waged against pagans simply because they were pagans. To this Sepúlveda agreed, following natural law as elucidated by St. Thomas Aquinas, and interpreted by his followers. But when Indian religions included human sacrifice, such as in New Spain where 20,000 innocent souls were purportedly sacrificed annually before the arrival of the Spanish, then force in the name of civilization and Christianity was justified. Sepúlveda drew upon the Old Testament as well as the New. "We can see where God gave the clearest indications for the extermination of these barbarians as witnessed by God giving the people of Israel the authority to exterminate the idolatrous Canaanites and Amorites."[6]

Sepúlveda extolled the virtues of Spanish civilization, having been given, by virtue of discovery and confirmed by the Papal Donation, the right to evangelize these barbarous peoples. Even though the Spanish people excelled in prudence, justice, religion, humanism, and in other sorts of virtue, there had been, Sepúlveda admitted, occasional excesses committed by some magistrates and evil subjects in the course of war. But, even admitting the existence of cruelty and avarice, this did not invalidate the legitimate empire of the prince, Charles, and his predecessors. Sepúlveda, like Las Casas, drew upon history to buttress his arguments.

The Roman Empire had been just, but even more just was the Spanish one, founded on Christian principles. There was nothing more salutary than for the barbarians to be brought under the rule of Charles Caesar [the Emperor Charles V] for he converted them into civilized men and gave them public precepts of law and letters, as well as religion and good customs. In the end, as Sepúlveda finished refining his humanistic doctrine, he wrote that the King needed to prevent any repetition of cruelties which are said to have happened, and he needs to ensure the well-being of his subjects and the liberty consistent with their nature and condition.[7]

This Euro-centric view tinged with racism was quite common to all European peoples of the sixteenth century—not only the Spanish and Portuguese, but also the English, French, and Dutch, as the century wore on and they too extended their claims to the New World. What stands out is Las Casas's challenge to this view, seeing the world more and from the other side, that of the native American peoples. In fact, as he grew older, he became even more intransigent in his principles, which came to include complete restitution of sovereignty and property to the Indians.

To settle the increasingly strident and public debate between Las Casas and Sepúlveda, the Council of the Indies stepped in with a firm recommendation and declared that the dangers to both the Indians and to the King's conscience by the conquests were so great that no new expedition ought to be licensed without his express permission and that of the Council. Moreover, the Council concluded, a meeting of theologians and jurists was needed to discuss "how conquests may be conducted justly and with security of conscience."[8] Charles concurred, and, as noted, on April 16, 1550, ordered all conquests in the Indies be suspended.

Probably never before, or since, one of the great modern students of Las Casas, Lewis Hanke, wrote, has a mighty emperor—and in 1550 Charles V was the strongest ruler in Europe, with a great overseas empire besides—ordered his conquests to cease until it was decided if they were just.[9] This special council convened in August, 1550, in Valladolid and they asked Sepúlveda and Las Casas to present the arguments.

Sepúlveda started in mid-August, 1550, with a spirited three-hour defense of the conquest. Las Casas responded with a numbing five-day reading, word for word, of his 500 page—give or take a few pages—tract, "The Defense of … Las Casas … Against the Persecutors and Slanderers of the Peoples of the New World Discovered Across the Seas." He read the entire piece in what Lewis Hanke described as a "verbal onslaught." Neither Las Casas nor Sepúlveda attended the sessions where the other spoke.

The judges retired to consider the issues. Overwhelmed by Las Casas's arguments, they asked one of their members, the Dominican Domingo de Soto, to prepare a summary of the cases, proving that even sixteenth-century bureaucrats liked to simplify complex matters.

Soto prepared the summary, adding Sepúlveda's reply to twelve major objections Las Casas had raised in his original presentation. Both Sepúlveda and Las Casas were satisfied with the objective summary prepared by Soto. The next session did not occur until April and May, 1551, when the judges reconvened at Valladolid for the second, and last, time. In the meantime, Sepúlveda discovered, much to his disgust, that Las Casas had prepared an extensive rebuttal to Sepúlveda's replies.[10]

We do not know the final decision of the judges. Six or seven years later the Council of the Indies was still trying to obtain and compile the individual opinions of the judges. Meanwhile, both Las Casas and Sepúlveda claimed victory. The records of the council, if they exist, have never been discovered. While the issues were perhaps too complex to render a simple judgment, it was generally held that the conquests, to be legal, had to be done within a Christian context with due respect for the Indians, whatever that meant.

While critics of Las Casas accuse him of gross distortion, exaggeration, and fanaticism in defense of his cause (all of which is true), Sepúlveda and his supporters stretched the truth and distorted reality with equal abandon. Hernán Cortés, the conquistador of Mexico, shone in Sepúlveda's light. "Can there be a greater or stronger testimony how some men surpass others in talent, industry, strength of mind, and valor?," Sepúlveda asked rhetorically. "Or that other peoples are slaves by nature?"[11] By applying the calculus of comparison, the Indians fell deeper into the abyss of barbarity and inferiority spun by Sepúlveda to sustain his arguments.

"Nothing shows more of the crudity, barbarism, and native slavery of these men," said Sepúlveda, "than making known their institutions." "They certainly have homes, some manner of community living, and commerce," he admitted, "but what do homes, community living, and commerce prove except that they are not bears or monkeys and that they are not completely devoid of reason?"[12]

In this same vein, Sepúlveda continued triumphantly: "Shall we doubt that those peoples, so uncivilized, so barbarous, so wicked, contaminated with so many evils and wicked religious practices, have been justly subjugated by an excellent, pious, and most just King, such as was Ferdinand and the Emperor Charles is now, and by a most civilized nation that is outstanding in every kind of virtue?"[13]

After the first rush of the debate which lasted about two years, Sepúlveda grew tired of defending himself against Las Casas, "since there was no need to repeat something a thousand times, as he does," and he retired from the fray.[14]

In dealing with human sacrifice, Las Casas admitted that the Indians were "in probable error" in this area.[15] He concluded that sacrificing was part of universal worship in all religions, but that the Indians simply went too far in sacrificing human beings, their most valuable possession. His reasoning was convoluted and, in virtually any way of judging it, erroneous, both in its syllogistic structure and in its violation of basic Judeo-Christian doctrine. He lamely referred often in the course of his arguments to God's command to Abraham to sacrifice his son Isaac, but then forgets the whole purpose of that exercise: not to sacrifice Isaac, but to test Abraham's faith. Other passages in the Old Testament confirm God's condemnation of human sacrifice. Apart from human sacrifice, Las Casas's arguments were usually powerful, and he often harkened back to his formative early experiences on Española. And he was unrelenting in denying the validity of force in the evangelization of pagans. In a striking set of rhetorical questions, he defined the issues based on a profound understanding of Scripture.

"Now if Christians unsettle everything by wars, burnings, fury, rashness, fierceness, sedition, plunder, and insurrection, where is meekness?" he asked.[16]

"Where is moderation?"

"Where are the holy deeds that should move the hearts of pagans to glorify God?"

"Where is the blameless and inoffensive way of life?"

"Where is humanity?"

"Finally, where is the meek and gentle spirit of Christ?"

"Where is the imitation of Christ and Paul?"[17]

In his summary in the debate, the life and force of Las Casas's convictions emerge in a powerful voice. "The Indians are our brothers," he wrote, "and Christ has given his life for them" just as much as Christ laid it down his for his Jewish brothers (and, ultimately, all humankind) fifteen hundred years earlier.[18] If the Apostles Paul and Peter took the gospel to the Gentiles, in peace and friendship, then why should Indians be treated differently?

The issues raised at Valladolid in 1550–1551 transcend the fundamental ones of the justness of the conquest and the nature of American Indians. The very legitimacy of the Spanish to sovereignty over the Indies was called into question. If a just war was not waged against American Indians, then claims to sovereignty were mere usurpations, and there was no just title to the Indies. Here Las Casas and his supporters had to tread lightly. Espousing the cause of the Indians sat well on the conscience of Charles V. Calling the claims of his grandfather and grandmother (Ferdinand and Isabel) to the Indies false and illegal patently made his own claims to sovereignty, jurisdiction, and authority weak and theoretically untenable.

But the Conquest was reality. The academics and jurists could debate the issues, but, practically, there was no going back. Las Casas resigned his bishopric of Chiapa in the summer of 1550, and in 1552 he was off to Seville, not content to rest his case, but rather determined to keep battling for the very lives and souls of the American Indians by publishing many tracts, booklets, and books.

And, as he waged his lifelong war on behalf of Amerindians, he gradually changed his mind on one other great issue that had darkened his life: the trade in African slaves to the Americas, and on the institution of slavery itself.

Bartolomé de las Casas and the African slave trade

In 1516, to preserve the rapidly dwindling Taino population of the island of Española, Las Casas suggested importing some black and white slaves from Castile. He has been pilloried ever since for hypocritically advocating the initiation of the African slave trade in defense of American

Indians. What did Las Casas really advocate? Was he the first to do so as so many have claimed? Did he sustain and defend his advocacy of the slave trade over the years? If there ever was an issue that lends itself to different points of view, this is it.[19]

Since the first half of the fifteenth century, the Portuguese had been exploring the west coast of Africa. Just before mid-century they arrived in the area of Senegal and captured some Africans to be brought back to Portugal and sold into slavery.[20] Soon thereafter they discovered that it was more efficient, less confrontational, and quite a bit safer to deal directly with African kings and chiefs along the coast and up the rivers of West Africa and buy slaves offered for sale by the Africans themselves.

The Portuguese slave trade took advantage of a domestic slave system already well developed in West Africa. African slavery was very much in existence and flourishing in such pre-colonial African empires as Dahomey and Ashanti (modern Benin and Ghana).[21]

> The slave trade (and the Atlantic trade in general) should not be seen as an "impact" brought in from outside and functioning as some sort of autonomous factor in African history. Instead, it grew out of and was rationalized by the African societies who participated in it and had complete control over it until the slaves were loaded onto European ships for transfer to Atlantic societies.[22]

Basically the Portuguese trafficked in people already in bondage, thus making the slave trade a "just" trade and legal within the accepted norms of the age. By the time the young Las Casas reached the Indies for the first time in 1502, the Portuguese had been importing African slaves into Iberia for half a century. Many were carried to Portugal and southern Spain where they were employed in domestic service in urban centers such as Seville, where Las Casas was born and grew up.

While Europeans did not significantly change African slavery in the first century of the trade, the trade that eventually grew to supply the needs of American plantations was a new phenomenon. The transatlantic crossings and the rise of chattel slavery—especially in the English and French Caribbean colonies—transformed the slave trade and slavery itself from the relatively benign institution that existed in early Iberia to the plantation slavery of the Americas that was so inhumane and degrading.

The slaves in southern Iberia were rarely used in agriculture or plantation slavery as developed in the Americas. Rather they fit into society much like the Moorish slaves who preceded them, eventually being absorbed into the local society, becoming members of Christian brotherhoods, developing a significant free colored population, and these "African slaves readily adopted the culture, language, and religion of their masters."[23]

How conscious was the boy Las Casas of African slaves in his hometown of Seville? They may have represented at least 10 percent of the population by the early sixteenth century.[24] They were certainly visible and accepted as a part of the local scene, working in urban industries, going to church, forming part of the general population, not particularly deprived, oppressed, or stripped of much of their humanity as would occur in the plantations of the Americas by the eighteenth century. They were well acculturated into early modern Hispanic society and there was even a small but significant element of free blacks in the population, manumitted by either owners or having bought their way to freedom through Spain's slave codes. Meanwhile, on the large islands of the Spanish Caribbean, the Amerindians were reeling under the double onslaught of conquest and disease.

So, around 1517, some enterprising settlers suggested that "if we could each get licenses to bring a few dozen Negro slaves from Spain or Africa," it would alleviate the burden on the Indians.[25] There were already a few Africans on the island of Española—some slave and some free—and the sugar industry was underway, sugar cane having been imported as early as Columbus's voyages at the end of the fifteenth century. It was a natural fit, especially as the Indians were dying off in disastrous numbers and sugar fetched a good price in Europe.

Las Casas picked up on the idea, and, back in Spain in 1517–1519, he suggested to young King Charles's counselors that a license be issued to import Negro slaves directly from Spain or Africa to the islands. Later on he reflected on this.

This suggestion to issue a license to bring Negro slaves to the Indies was made first by the cleric Casas. Las Casas wrote in the third person, not seeing how unjust the Portuguese were in taking slaves on the coast of Africa. And then he added what would become the key to his thinking: "Later on he realized how unjustly and tyrannically Africans were taken slaves, in the same fashion as Indians."²⁶ Las Casas was quite honest in his admission of shortsightedness; and second, he was totally devoted to the Indians, so much so that he failed initially to see the implications of advocating licenses to import African slaves.²⁷

Las Casas later was sorry for all of this, for his initial motivation was to improve the lives of impoverished Spaniards on the islands, and, of course, to obtain the freedom of the Indians. In the end, the Spaniards made out okay, but the Indians remained "in captivity until there were none left to kill," and black slavery spread like a stain across the New World.²⁸ What had started out as a small effort to reduce the suffering of the Amerindians turned into a growing trade in human beings from Africa directly to the plantations of the Americas. Until near mid-century, he continued to espouse the introduction of African slaves, already in Spain or directly from the African coast, as a way of relieving the oppression and lifting the harsh and killing demands on the Indians.

What was Las Casas thinking when he suggested importing African slaves? Was it not grossly hypocritical to suggest alleviating the pain on the Amerindians and translating it to the backs of Africans?

The answer is that Las Casas was thinking of African slavery as he knew it from his childhood, growing up in Seville and its environs. It was not the degrading form of plantation slavery later developed by European planters in other parts of the Americas in the seventeenth and eighteenth centuries. It was an urban form of slavery, with Africans well integrated into the local society of Andalucia, with their religious brotherhoods, acculturated to Spanish, practicing crafts and skills in the community, some, in fact, becoming freedmen. Furthermore, slavery was part of life in the early sixteenth century, an accepted form of servitude since ancient times, and unquestioned by anyone—theologians, philosophers, statesmen, anyone who spoke with authority in the community. Yet, curiously enough, Las Casas, different from most of his contemporaries, did turn on the slave trade later in life, long before the morality of the slave trade—and African slavery in the Americas itself—was challenged by abolitionists almost two hundred years later.

At mid-century, as Las Casas studied the documents of the early period of discovery, as he pored over the reports of voyages by merchants and navigators in the service of Portugal and Spain—such as Christopher Columbus himself—to Guinea, to the Congo, to the Canary Islands, he began to perceive the nature of African slavery in its true dimensions.

"The Portuguese," Las Casas wrote, "had made a career in much of the past of raiding Guinea and enslaving blacks, absolutely unjustly. When they saw that the Spanish sugar planters and sugar mill operators on the islands had such a need of blacks and that they sold for high prices, the Portuguese speeded up their slave raiding. They took slaves in every evil and wicked way they could. And the Africans themselves, when they saw the Portuguese so eagerly on the hunt for slaves, used unjust wars and other lawless means to steal and sell to the Portuguese."[29]

And we, Las Casas reflected, not about to excuse the Spaniards, are the cause of all the sins the one and the other commit, in addition to what we commit in buying them.[30] Las Casas was persuaded to denounce the African slave trade from his experience as an eyewitness in the Indies, and from the documentary record preserved by Portuguese chroniclers that he was now reading at mid-century in Seville.

Las Casas was particularly moved by the chronicle of the first Portuguese slaving expeditions to Africa in 1444 written by the Portuguese Gómez Eanes de Zurara.[31] It is a story filled with cruelty and sadness. On his return to Spain in 1547, Las Casas had picked up in Lisbon some manuscripts, chronicles, and books on the Portuguese expansion into the Atlantic and down the African coast. Eanes de Zurara recorded the division of families, children stripped from parents, mothers clinging to their toddlers, husbands divided from wives. Some family members could scarcely be pried apart, their faces wet with tears, crying aloud for succor, lashed by the overseers. As Eanes recalled in a callous phrase, "the partition took a lot of trouble."[32]

Eanes attempted to excuse this pitiful scene by emphasizing that, at least, the Africans were brought to Christianity in subsequent years. He seemed, Las Casas weighed in, "only a little less foolish than the Infante [Prince Henry the Navigator], unable to see that neither the Infante's good intentions [Henry refused to take possessions of his slaves, but allowed them to be taken by others to preserve 'his good conscience'], nor the good results that later followed [conversion], excused the sins of violence, the deaths, the damnation of those who perished without faith or sacrament, the enslavement of the survivors."[33]

Las Casas continued in the same vein carrying the argument to its logical conclusion: nor did Henry's good intentions or conversion make up for the monumental injustice. What love, affection, esteem, reverence would they have, Las Casas asked in a moving passage, "could they have for the faith, for Christian religion, so as to covert to it, those who wept as they did, who grieved, who raised their eyes, their hands to heaven, who saw themselves, against of the law of nature, against all human reason, stripped of their liberty, of their wives and children, of their homeland, of their peace?"[34]

Las Casas, the man who screened and measured the actions of Christians through Scripture and natural law, saw *no* mitigating circumstance that could assuage the monstrosity of the growing slave trade. Recall, this was also Las Casas the polemicist, who had been sharpening his skills chastising and condemning a whole generation of Spaniards for despoiling the Amerindians of their liberty, their property, and their very lives, much the same as Europeans were now doing to Africans.

While the legitimacy of slavery as an institution was hardly questioned during Las Casas's lifetime, what divided scholars and philosophers was the question of a just war.[35] If declared "just," then the enslavement of prisoners and captives was acceptable. If the war was not just, as Las Casas claimed in attacking all violence done on the Indians, then the taking of captives and enslaving them were illegal.

Some did question the Portuguese enslavement of Africans. Were they captured in just wars? Could Christians engage in any war deemed "just" since all wars were wrapped in violence, and Jesus Christ, at the very core of Christianity, did not condone the use of violence? Or did he?

Many Christian scholars followed St. Augustine in the question of just war. While war is a sin, it could be construed as acceptable if somehow waged by the state to right some wrongs.[36] Secondarily, but no less important, was whether force could be used in evangelization. There were often wide margins dividing the two points of view. Some agreed with Augustine; others just as emphatically denied his position. Those who defended it—usually gingerly like Augustine—did so by employing Scripture, such as the parable of the wedding feast, which could be construed as requiring compulsion/force to spread the Gospel.

Figure 6.1   This original painting of Las Casas is one of the few authentic portraits, done sometime between 1548 and 1556, or about the time he recanted from his earlier endorsement of the African slave trade and instead condemned it, and African slavery in general, at the end of his life.

To Las Casas, the author of *The Only Way* of true evangelization, it seemed increasingly clear that neither rationalization—just war *or* the use of force—could be invoked to take and sell slaves. *The Only Way* was peaceful evangelization, no matter the circumstances, the place, or the state of the recipients. They were all born free—at least in principle, according to natural law—and their conversion had to be freely solicited and freely given. Otherwise it was a fraud and contrary to Scripture.

The argument that enslavement was a natural step to Christianity was dismissed contemptuously by another contemporary of Las Casas, Bartolomé de Albornoz, a Dominican who taught at one time at the University of Mexico. In his *Arte de los contratos* (1573), Albornoz questioned

> the alleged justifications for slavery (war, conviction of a crime, purchase) ... [and] against those who were saying that enslaved blacks actually profited in the balance, since they received the Christian faith, [Albornoz] replied that according to the law of Jesus Christ the soul's freedom may not be purchased with the body's enslavement.[37]

It took the passage of time, however, for Las Casas to come to this same view. He continued to advocate the introduction of African slaves from 1517 to at least near mid-century. Various petitions and letters, dating from 1518, 1531, and lastly in 1543, all suggested or requested that slaves be shipped to the Indies.

A dramatic about-face took place in his attitude towards slavery and the slave trade at mid-century. Before then Las Casas merely mirrored the prevailing philosophical and social currents of his age, which accepted slavery pretty much unconditionally as a form of natural servitude. But then something happened: "After his last involvement in the matter (1543), things began to change ... We have forthright, painful documents expressing his repentance for the blindness in which he had lived up to the middle of the sixteenth century."[38]

On advocating the importation of slaves back in 1516, Las Casas wrote that he regretted the advice he gave the King on this matter. He judged himself culpable through inadvertence—when he saw proven that the enslavement of blacks was every bit as unjust as that of the Indians. And as he thought it through, he offered that it was not, in any case, a good solution he had proposed, that blacks be brought in so Indians could be freed. And this even as he thought that the blacks had been justly enslaved. And he admitted that he was not certain that his ignorance and his good intentions would excuse him before the judgment seat of God.[39] This is a key and powerful admission of wrong and a demonstration of profound repentance.

What produced such a profound change? It flowed from three major sources. One was Scripture. How could one reconcile the love of Jesus Christ with the inhumanity of the slave trade? The second was the testimony of the Portuguese chroniclers themselves, especially Gómez Eanes, whose accounts were heart-rending. And the third was Las Casas's own experience with slavery, both Indian and African. What was different was that at this point in his life he was beginning to conflate the Indian experience of slavery with the African one.

It is clear from the following passage that Las Casas considered Indian slavery and African slavery in the same breath. Both were illegal and tyrannical.

> This note to give license to bring black slaves to these lands was first given by the cleric Casas, not taking into account the injustice with which the Portuguese captured and enslaved them; then, having discovered this, he would not for all the world advocate this, for he held enslaving them both unjust and tyrannical; and the same goes for the Indians.[40]

Once Las Casas accepted the truth that the African slaves in the plantations and mines of the Indies were as equally oppressed as the Indians, then it was but one step further to denounce not only the slave trade, but also African slavery itself, which was a big step far beyond the accepted norms in the sixteenth century.

Las Casas left no doubt where his sympathies lay. He discovered in the Portuguese chronicles of the slave trade all the evidence he needed to pronounce Portuguese behavior illegal, immoral, and plain horrific. He contemptuously dismissed the "we-did-this-to-covert-them-to-Christianity" excuse as a pitiful defense of a heinous crime.

His conclusion to Chapter Twenty-Four in the first volume of his *History* recounts exactly where he stood on the issue of the Portuguese enslavement of Africans to send to the Indies. Las Casas wrote that even the historian himself [Gómez Eanes], and the people who stood around, wept with compassion over the sorry affair, especially when they saw the separation of children from parents, of mothers and fathers from children.[41]

Las Casas continued in this vein: "It is obvious of the error, the self-deception of those people back then … The historian [again Eanes] shows the event to be the horror that it is," though later he seems to soft-soap it, to blur it with the mercy and goodness of God. If anything good did come of it later, Las Casas added almost resignedly, it all came from God. What came from Prince Henry and the raiders he sent out was brutality, theft, tyranny—nothing more.[42]

While the Portuguese are held to account in the main, he does not spare fellow Spaniards whose greed in fact drove the slave trade. Spanish interests, he wrote, motivated the slavers. And, as usual, he also analyzed: greed is infectious, with the result that the Africans themselves began to wage unjust wars and employ other illicit ways to take slaves and sell them to the Portuguese, who then transported them across the Atlantic to be sold in the Spanish and Portuguese (largely Brazil) plantations of the New World.[43]

At the core of the illegal and inhumane slave trade, Las Casas, the Christian missionary friar, laid the blame squarely on sin, of which greed and cupidity of course are two of the most egregious transgressions of God's commandments.

As we examine points of view in this volume, we need to ask the question: did Las Casas condemn slavery across the board as an evil as strongly and clearly he condemned the slave trade? These are two related, but distinct issues. He had no problem in labeling the slave trade evil and illegal: evil within the context of Christian doctrine and illegal within the Thomistic doctrine of natural law that all men are born free, and deserve to remain free. Las Casas extended his doctrinal defense of Indians to the slave trade. It is quite apparent that his condemnation of the slave trade extended to slavery itself, placing Las Casas awkwardly against the norms of his age, since the abolitionist movement is not thought to have begun until the eighteenth century.[44]

That it put him at odds with prevailing sentiments, legal traditions, and contemporary practices weighed little on his balance of doing what he thought was right or wrong. He sought justice, and true justice was blind to race, to nationality, to whether one was pagan or Christian. The man often pilloried for advocating, hypocritically, the initiation of the African slave trade was instead one of the philosophical and spiritual progenitors of the abolitionist movement that sprang to life a century and a half after he died.[45]

Contemporaneously with his change of heart and mind on the African slave trade, he resigned in 1550 as Bishop and turned to the job of publishing many of his works to extend their influence. He did this in Seville in 1552, where he had gone to oversee the sailing of Dominicans he had recruited to send to the Indies. Seville was one of the publishing centers of Spain, and Las Casas published eight of his major treatises while there.

There may have been a ninth tract which was suppressed by the Inquisition at the possible instigation of Sepúlveda. This work was entitled *Erudita et elegans explicatio*, a long treatise in Latin which contains some of the principal doctrinal bases for many Las Casas's claims and accusations. The *Erudita* treatise was denounced to the Inquisition in 1552 "as contrary to the doctrine of Saint Peter and Saint Paul about the subjection of serfs and vassals to their lords and kings."[46] Las Casas was vexed by this accusation but the Inquisition did not follow through beyond seizing the manuscript in 1552.

It is not clear who denounced Las Casas before the Inquisition, but quite probably it was Sepúlveda, chagrined by Las Casas's continuing intemperate accusations. He accused Las Casas of heresy and *lesé-majesté*, having directly contradicted the teachings of St. Paul and St. Peter, presumably those dealing with obeying civil authority. In Chapter Thirteen of Paul's letter to the Romans, especially verses 1–7 and Peter's First Letter, verses 13–14, both Apostles urge Christians to submit to established authority. They are not passages without controversy. What if a tyrant rules? Are Christians to obey evil men who come to power, either through birth as in ancient times, or through manipulation and guile as in modern times? The Inquisition in fact did little with Sepúlveda's accusation. They received the denunciation and this ninth work was not published until after Las Casas's death, but they did not take on the Bishop of Chiapa directly.

The two most polemical pieces were the *Brief History of the Destruction of the Indies*, and his rules for confessors, the *Confesionario*. The *Brief History* was essentially an abridgement of the worst atrocities committed by the Spaniards in the Conquest, and, hence, the basis for the "Black Legend." The *Confesionario* contained the twelve "rules" for confessors, probably the most controversial piece that Las Casas ever wrote, and which caused him the most trouble in his lifetime. If these rules were not followed, priests were instructed to deny confession and absolution, even to dying men.

In general, the basic premise of all these writings was that since the *encomienda* and the conquest in general had stripped the Indians of what was rightfully theirs (dominion, freedom, material goods, and, ultimately, their lives in millions of cases), it was necessary for Spaniards to repent and restore what had been taken, or the Christians were lost forever. Their eternal salvation was at stake. If *encomenderos*, old conquistadors, civil officials, and others, on their deathbeds, failed to comply with the rules for confessors, for example, they were doomed. Many, in fact, did make deathbed confessions and provided for restitution, but the rules were not universally accepted throughout the Indies.

When the treatises reached New Spain, one of Las Casas's most insistent critics, the Franciscan Motolinía, wrote a famous letter to the Emperor in 1555 and demanded that Las Casas be locked up in a monastery. The Cabildo of Mexico City met on December 29, 1553, and, along with most of the leading officials and *encomenderos*, prohibited the circulation of the *Brief History*.

In the *Brief History* Las Casas loosened whatever self-control he might have been inclined to impose on his writings, and spawned a condemnation of Spanish brutality and cruelty in the conquest of the Indies that still sears the mind and heart. It was the one work that ensured his fame, or infamy, for the next five hundred years. Translated into other languages, it became the cornerstone of the Black Legend wherein English and Dutch publicists, propagandists, and Protestants impaled Spaniards and Catholics (synonymous in the superheated religious debates that escalated into religious warfare in the sixteenth century) for extreme cruelty and barbarity in the treatment of Amerindians. It is both his most controversial and exaggerated account. Alvaro Huerga, a sympathetic modern biographer, and a Dominican like Las Casas, wrote of the *Brief History*:

From the rational point of view it is much inferior to the *History of the Indies* and the *Apologética Historia*. It is a journalistic piece, without a rigorous methodology, without proof of its claims: the only document he inserts is an anonymous piece of a letter which agrees with him, without the least identification of source or guarantee of its legitimacy. Its point

of view is horrific, Bartolomé de las Casas's most famous libel, the cornerstone of the "Black Legend," the nail used by Protestant Argonauts in
their condemnation of Spanish colonization ... the tree from which everyone, each reader and each interpreter, hews the firewood he wants.[47]

In its content the *Brief History* is entirely negative. There are no redeeming qualities in the Spanish character in this polemic. It reflected Las
Casas's agitated state of mind when first drafted in 1542, and, perhaps,
even a temporary depression in 1552, having failed as Bishop of Chiapa
and with no clear victory in his various exchanges with Sepúlveda in
1550–1551.

His descriptions were rough, unpolished, calling for compassion for
the oppressed. They proclaimed the true missionary spirit that Spaniards
should follow in the Indies if they wanted to live at peace with their
conscience. His writings, freighted with repetitive arguments, wore down
his opponents, if not with his rationale, then with his insistence, never
yielding to not having the last word in any debate. While a sense of
humor was not part of Las Casas's persona, he was capable of irony and
he used it to wilt his opponents and persuade his readers. In a memorial
sent to the court on October 15, 1535, he referred to "Pizarro and his
saintly disciples" as the savages who murdered the Emperor Atahualpa
and were despoiling Peru.[48]

While his writing was furious and often rough, he was capable of
eloquence and noble sentiments expressed in moving prose. On war, he
wrote:

> War brings with it evils: the clash of arms; sudden, impetuous and furious
> invasions and attacks; violence and butchery; destruction, ruin, robbery
> ... War brings sadness to homes, everyone filled with fear, sobs, laments,
> and wailing. Artisans fall behind; the poor are plunged into fasting to
> survive or giving themselves to evil ways; the rich deplore goods stolen or
> fear for what they still have ... Weddings cease to be held, or are melan-
> choly events; women, desolated by war, are barren. Laws fall silent;
> humanitarian sentiments are laughed at; there is no justice or mercy
> anywhere.[49]

While in Seville in 1552, he also had access to the Columbus family
archives in a chapel of the local Carthusian monastery. This was a

historian's dream.[50] There, with all the Columbus documents at hand and made available to him by the family, Las Casas continued to rewrite his massive *History of the Indies*. The Columbus papers included the library of the late Hernando Columbus (Columbus's illegitimate second son). Hernando had not only produced a biography of his father which Las Casas consulted, but he also found the abridged version of Columbus's original log of the first voyage. Little did Las Casas know that he would be the last to see this historic document and the last to copy it, which he did to include in his *History*. It is the only record of this precious log which we have, since the original and several early copies disappeared.

While he worked on his *History*, Las Casas also broke out portions of it, later to be published separately as *Apologetica Historica*, or *Defensive or Explanatory History*. While the *History of the Indies* took a narrative approach, the *Apologetica* was more of a natural, descriptive history of the area and its people, describing habits, flora, fauna, nature, foods, geography, and just about anything else that crossed Las Casas's horizon. It was composed to elevate Indian culture and civilization and rate it comparably to Spanish civilization.

His life was punctuated by controversy as always, none perhaps more dramatic than his scraps with the powerful Inquisition. In 1559, he took the side of his close friend and fellow Dominican, Bartolomé de Carranza de Miranda (1503–1576), then Archibishop of Toledo and primate of Spain, who was denounced to the Inquisition and underwent the most sensational trial of the century. Few stood by Carranza de Miranda since not only the Inquisition but also Philip II attempted to destroy him. It took courage and a formidable reputation to stand up both to King and Inquisition. Some of Las Casas's works were denounced to the Inquisition, but nothing came of these charges and Las Casas was never himself condemned or called before a tribunal.

While Las Casas occasionally jousted with the Inquisition, another mortal challenge engaged him more directly. In the early 1550s, the *encomenderos* of Peru lobbied hard with Prince Philip to grant their *encomiendas* in perpetuity. Las Casas's lifelong goal was to abolish the *encomienda*, and the Peruvian conquistadors wished to extend it forever, from son to son down through the ages. The arguments, and the battle between Las Casas and the Peruvian *encomenderos*, were long and involved, and occupied his attention until his death in 1566. For Las

Casas, the Peruvian *encomenderos* were the villains, and the dispossessed Inca rulers the victims of a monstrous injustice. The *encomenderos* should be stripped of their illegally-gained power and goods, and the Inca rulers restored to their place of authority before the arrival of the Spaniards. This was the theory of restitution carried to its ultimate conclusion.

The battles around these issues are fascinating. In 1554–1555, for example, Philip was in England preparing for his marriage to the zealous Catholic Queen Mary. From there he dealt with affairs in his far-flung empire, which included the proposal of perpetuity by the Peruvian *encomenderos*. Antonio de Ribera, the Peruvians' representative to the Court, had arrived in England early in 1555 and offered Philip a fabulous sum, seven to nine million ducats, in return for granting perpetual *encomiendas*. Strapped for money, Philip was tempted.

Las Casas jumped on this menace with characteristic alacrity. If the *encomenderos* got away with this, it would finish their destruction of the Indians within the old Inca Empire. Las Casas never shied from hyperbole. His reaction was typically Lascasian—impetuous, uncompromising, Satanizing his opponents, and championing his cause with absolute conviction. Las Casas appealed to his old Dominican friend, Bartolomé Carranza de Miranda, Philip's confessor in England, to intercede and persuade Philip not to make a hasty decision. Carranza was persuasive, but Philip needed the money.

Sometime in 1556, Philip ordered his Council of the Indies to accept the offer of the Peruvian *encomenderos*. The offer was too tempting. This, in turn, threw Las Casas into high gear. He gathered his allies and persuaded the Peruvian Indians to make a counter-offer. They would match anything the *encomenderos* could muster and buy their freedom—and Las Casas questioned that the Spanish *encomenderos* could come even close to raising the bounty they promised.

Then the weight of bureaucracy ground Philip's decision to a slow halt. The King ordered commissioners sent to Peru to examine the issue. The Council of the Indies took two years to select appropriate ones. After investigating the issue in Peru, the commissioners returned and rendered their decision. There were no clear victors. Some of the *encomenderos*— the first conquistadors of Peru, for example—were confirmed perpetually, others only for a lifetime, and other *encomiendas* reverted to the

Crown. There was no wholesale confirmation of all *encomiendas* in perpetuity. Las Casas won this last war, but in the "treaties" he had to yield in some areas.

In 1561, Las Casas moved to the Dominican monastery at Atocha in Madrid where he remained active, corresponding with fellow clergy, largely Dominicans, across the Americas, arguing his causes with energy and conviction. They sought his advice and counsel, and he responded with vigor, this oldest protector of American Indians. He passed away July 18, 1566, and was buried two days later. Busy until the end, Las Casas penned a long letter to a fellow Dominican, the new Pope, Pius V, earlier that year, calling upon him to take up the challenge of rectifying the errors of the Conquest. And, just a few days before his death, he presented a long memorial to the Council of the Indies, describing and defending his positions, advocating radical reforms—restitution of all Indian properties, restoration of Indian sovereignty—that would never come about.

Las Casas had, in fact, outlived the reformist, Millenarian spirit of earlier years that had so permeated the Catholic Church in Spain. His soul and his pen, however, never quieted in pursuit of justice for the Indians. Yet, while the Spanish occupation of the Indies was a fact, future expeditions—into Florida, into northern Mexico, into New Mexico, and into other frontiers of the Empire as it was taking shape—carried disclaimers and clauses protecting the Indians. Philip II issued royal ordinances in 1573 that codified these provisions in a belated testimony to Las Casas's legacy.

Conclusion

I have fought the good fight, I have finished the race, I have kept the faith.
2 Timothy 4:7

There is no more fitting epigraph to the life of Bartolomé de las Casas. It is from the Apostle Paul's letter to his young associate Timothy, written towards the end of Paul's life. It speaks eloquently to faithfulness, a quality which Las Casas demonstrated his entire life to the cause of justice and truth as he saw it. Las Casas always thought of himself as the shepherd to the Indians of the New World, while his detractors viewed him as the enemy of everything that was good and noble in the Spanish character. If there was ever a clash of points of view, it was in defining Las Casas's life and cause.

Over his long life, Las Casas achieved one extraordinary goal: lifting the American Indian before the Spanish, and European, conscience. He sought to give voice to those conquered, to lift them before the highest tribunals in the land, and render justice. He did so with passion and conviction, his own voice rising to the level of kings and emperors, seeking redress for the wrongs and sins committed by several generations of his countrymen.

In doing so, he pioneered a new understanding of human rights, based on the extraordinary discovery of a new world and a new people that challenged Europeans to accommodate to a part of the universe they

Bartolomé de las Casas and the Conquest of the Americas. Lawrence A. Clayton
© 2011 Lawrence A. Clayton

knew nothing of before Columbus returned to Spain in the winter of 1492–1493. Las Casas lifted the American Indians into the cosmos of Christian theology, and in doing so helped pave the way to an understanding that indeed all humankind is one.

Las Casas's detractors also have a powerful and, sometimes, persuasive voice at the table of historical judgment. Their principal criticism was his obsession—some would say Satanic possession—with defending the Indians. To do so Las Casas indicted entire generations of Spaniards who conquered and settled the Americas. Others frame his obsession in more quasi-scientific terms, such as Menéndez Pidal, who labeled him a paranoic, driven by a vision that viewed all Spanish achievements in this period as evil. From this premise, Las Casas, suffering from "prophetic delusions," launched his lifelong of vilification of everything Hispanic.

Today the Conquest is sometimes referred to as the Encounter, for many good reasons, but a conquest it was, and Las Casas was seared for life by the brutality he had witnessed as a young man on Española and Cuba. Yet he was not without compassion for many of his fellow countrymen who had not fared so well in the Indies, who were not the great *encomenderos* and conquistadors. He favored them in some of his proposed legislation, perhaps seeing in their poverty and lack of circumstances a reflection of the suffering of American Indians. He also took compassion on the blacks captured in Africa and brought over in the lucrative slave trade, even though he had been one of its early proponents, again, blinded by his determination to bring justice and freedom to the Indians.

He triggered the Black Legend with the publication of his *Brief History* and that Legend became one of the cornerstones of the titanic struggle between Protestant and Catholics in the succeeding centuries. Yet he also preserved the diary of Columbus's first voyage, a priceless document from the age of exploration and discovery, in his monumental *History of the Indies*.

He defended his friends, such as Bartolomé Carranza de Miranda, before the Inquisition, with courage and devotion. Yet he also persuaded his old mentor, Domingo de Betanzos, to make a deathbed retraction and confession that raised the eyebrows of many in the ecclesiastical community. Las Casas could, in fact, be merciless when it came to defending the Indians, even to the point of forcing Betanzos to repent as he died.

If a figure such as Hernán Cortés represents the essence of the Conquistador, then Bartolomé de las Casas was the quintessential anti-Conquistador. He not only struck at them for brutality and inhumanity, but also swept away the theoretical framework for claiming Spanish sovereignty and authority in the Indies. He, as others, called the Papal Donation of 1493 irrelevant and doctrinally in error, denounced the claims to sovereignty by virtue of "discovery" as self-serving, and labeled the behavior of the "Christians" as they swept across the Indies as barbaric, totally at odds with Scripture. Las Casas became the "counter-labeler," the one who probed deeply into the "other" (the Indian was, after all, the ultimate "other" for the ethnocentric Europeans), as he waged a lifelong war to see his views prevail, and, of course, to act on them.

He lived such a long life that he eventually outlived the early and powerful reformist millenarianism of his fellow Dominicans, Franciscans and Augustinians who shared his views. By the second half of the sixteenth century, leaders such as Philip II were moving on with the consolidation of empire and were less inclined than their fathers to consider radical changes, such as the wholesale restitution which Las Casas espoused at the end of his life.

While the immediate effect that Las Casas had on affairs waned, his legacy was guaranteed by the nature of his quest and his writings. He was, after all, devoted to such eternal concerns as truth and justice, which transcend time. One modern biographer, Gustavo Gutiérrez, has portrayed Las Casas as a precursor to the modern Liberation Theology movement that swept through Latin American Christendom in the second half of the twentieth century. And Las Casas's writings not only carried his arguments, but also left a richly endowed history of the early Spanish empire in the Indies. This was the dawn of modern American civilization as we know it, if by American we mean the whole of the American continents as many understood that term before the nineteenth century. And at its center, forming and reforming it, was Bartolomé de las Casas, protector of American Indians.

Notes

Introduction

1 John H. Parry, "Early European Penetration of Eastern North America," in R. Reid Badger and Lawrence A. Clayton, eds. *Alabama and the Borderlands: From Prehistory to Statehood* (Tuscaloosa, AL: University of Alabama Press, 1985), pp. 83–95.

2 Amerindian is a conflation of American and Indian and is used occasionally in this book following modern practice, although you will see Indian employed more frequently since this book is about the Americas, not the subcontinent of India in Asia.

3 "Nahua" is used more and more frequently by scholars writing about the Amerindians of central Mexico, but we have observed the traditional convention of "Aztec" since it is acceptable and easily recognizable. See "Notes on Sources and Conventions Used," in Stuart B. Schwartz, ed. and introduction, *Victors and Vanquished: Spanish and Nahua Views of the Conquest of Mexico* (Boston: Bedford/St. Martin's, 2000), pp. ix–x.

4 See, for example, George Raudzen "Outfighting or Outpopulating: Main Reasons for Early Colonial Conquests, 1493–1788," in George Raudzens, ed. and contributor, *Technology, Disease, and Colonial Conquests, Sixteenth to Eighteenth Centuries: Essays Reappraising the Guns and Germs Theories* (Leiden: Brill, 2001), pp. 31–57.

5 See Francis Brooks, "The Impact of Disease," in Raudzens, *Technology, Disease*, pp. 127–165.

6 See Matthew Restall, *Seven Myths of the Spanish Conquest* (New York: Oxford University Press, 2004) for an accessible presentation of some of these "myths" of the conquest.

7 Since Columbus thought he had found his way to Asia, and the "Indies," a kind of amorphous term that Europeans sometimes employed for Asia, or what they knew of it, Columbus referred to the islands he had found as part of the "Indies." The name stuck among Spaniards and for most of the colonial period, in Spanish documents, the Americas were often referred to as the Indies.

8 Bartolomé de las Casas, *Obras completas*, vol. V, p. 2160: "porque es una candela que todo lo encenderá."

9 Thomas Benjamin, *The Atlantic World: Europeans, Africans, Indians, and Their Shared History 1400–1900* (New York: Cambridge University Press, 2009). This and the following quote in text are from pp. xxv–xxvi and xxix, respectively. Benjamin's work is an excellent introduction to the Atlantic world.

10 See Fernando Cervantes, *The Devil in the New World: The Impact of Diabolism in New Spain* (New Haven, CT: Yale University Press, 1997) for a good example of modern literature exploring this theme.

11 A good discussion of the preservation and continuation of American culture is Chapter 6, "The Indians are Coming to an End: The Myth of Native Desolation," in Matthew Restall, *Seven Myths of the Spanish Conquest* (New York: Oxford University Press, 2003). Restall, in fact, presents a fairly balanced description, but fully integrates into his challenge of this myth many articles of "agency" faith.

12 Those who allied themselves with the Spanish to defeat ancient enemies of course welcomed these very good soldiers armed with steel and horses, but embracing the powerful ally who had helped you in combat was a dangerous business for even allies were looked upon with suspicion by the powerful and often duplicitous Spanish.

13 Stafford Poole, essay on "The Prophetic Personality in Scripture and History," contained in a personal communication (email) to L. Clayton, October, 2009. The essay was read at a conference at the University of Florida in the 1990s.

14 See Chapter 2.

15 Poole, essay on "The Prophetic Personality in Scripture and History."

16 You will find "chronicler" and/or "chronicle" used often interchangeably with historian and history in the story of Las Casas. He considered himself a historian, but since he wrote in a roughly chronological order, recording faithfully many of the events he either witnessed, heard about, or read

about, he is called a chronicler, whose root is the Greek work for "time." He was, in fact, both, chronicler and historian, one who analyzes and contextualizes the past, rather than simply recording as—in theory—a chronicler did. See L. A. Clayton "Teaching Las Casas through the Lens of the Historian," in Santa Arias and Eyda M. Merediz, eds. and contributors, *Approaches to Teaching the Writings of Bartolomé de las Casas* (New York: Modern Languages Association of America, 2008), pp. 33–41.

1   The era of Columbus and the "discoverers"

1   "Iberia" being the name of the entire peninsula under Roman rule.
2   Although Columbus did not achieve the celebrity or fame that history ascribed to him until several centuries later. In his lifetime, he was but one among a number of celebrated navigators and discoverers.
3   See L. A. Clayton, "The Iberian Advantage," in George Raudzen, ed, *Technology, Disease, and Colonial Conquests, Sixteenth to Eighteenth Centuries: Essays Reappraising the Guns and Germs Theory* (Leiden: Brill, 2001).
4   Peggy K. Liss, *Isabel the Queen: Life and Times* (New York: Oxford University Press, 1992), p. 331, quoting from Pedro Mártir, *Epistolario, epís.* 215.
5   Bartolomé de las Casas, *Apologética Historia Sumaria,* cáp. 49, in *Obras completas, Bartolomé de las Casas* (15 vols.: Madrid: Alianza, 1988–1998), vol. VII, p. 540.
6   George Sanderlin, *Las Casas: A Selection of His Writings* (New York: Alfred A. Knopf, 1971), pp. 6, 7; Henry Raup Wagner, in collaboration with Helen Rand Parish, *The Life and Writings of Las Casas* (Albuquerque: University of New Mexico Press, 1967), p. 16.
7   Las Casas, *Historia de Indias* (hereafter *HI*), Chap. 176, in *Obras completas* (hereafter *Obras*), vol. IV, p. 1243.
8   Las Casas, *HI.*
9   Las Casas, *HI.*
10   Las Casas, *HI.* This, and the remainder of the quotations, all recorded by Las Casas on pp. 1273–1274.
11   *HI*, I, Chap. 141, *Obras*, vol. IV, p. 1082.
12   The Black Legend is the source of much controversy. See the bibliographical essay at end of this book for a fuller discussion. A few of the most helpful works are Benjamin Keen, *Essays in the Intellectual History of Colonial Latin America* (Boulder, CO: Westview Press, 1998), Lewis Hanke, "More Heat and Some Light on the Spanish Struggle for Justice in the Conquest of America," *Hispanic American Historical Review* 44(3) (1964): 293–340, and

since Las Casas documented the conditions that precipitated the Black Legend, his own writings are immensely valuable as eye witness accounts. The latest version of Las Casas's seminal work on this subject, in English, with one of the best introductions is *An Account, Much Abbreviated, of the Destruction of the Indies, with Related Texts*, edited and with an introduction by Franklin W. Knight and translated by Andrew Hurley (Indianapolis, Indiana: Hackett Publishing, 2003).

13 This and other sections told by Las Casas in *HI*, *Obras*, vol. IV, pp. 1296ff.

14 *HI*, 2, Part III, Chap. 6, *Obras*, vol. IV, p. 1313.

15 Lynne Guitar, "Documenting the Myth of Taino Extinction," *Kacike: Journal of Caribbean Amerindian Archaeology and History* [On-line Journal], Special Issue, Lynne Guitar, Ed. Available at: http://www.kacike.org/GuitarEnglish.pdf, date of access: January 2, 2008. See also her "Criollos: The Birth of a Dynamic New Indo-Afro-European People and Culture on Española," *Kacike: Journal of Caribbean Amerindian History and Anthropology*, 1(1) (Jan. 2000–June 2000): 1–17.

16 *HI*, Book 2, Part 2, Chap. 7, *Obras*, vol. IV, pp. 1318–1319. All of the quotations and references to this incident that follow are taken from these two pages in Las Casas's *History of the Indies*.

17 Noble David Cook, *Born to Die: Disease and New World Conquest, 1492–1650* (New York: Cambridge University Press, 1998), p. 18.

18 *HI*, Book 2, Part III, section 6, Chapter 15 ff, *Obras*, vol. IV, pp. 1356–1371. Most of the following passages on the second Higüey campaign come from this section of *HI*. And, in fact, there do exist some large and impressive natural caves and caverns, especially in the Samaná Bay region of the island, either used or inhabited in some instances by the Tainos. I saw some of these on a mission trip to the island, June, 2009. For the most recent treatment of Fernández de Oviedo, see Kathleen Ann Myers, translations by Nina M. Scott, *Ferández de Oviedo's Chronicle of America: A New History for a New World* (Austin: University of Texas Press, 2007).

19 *HI*, Book 2, Part III, Section 6, Chapter 17, *Obras*, vol. IV, pp. 1363ff.

20 *HI*, Book 2, Part III, Section 6, Chapter 17, *Obras*, vol. IV, pp. 1363ff. This and following quotes from here.

21 Lynne Guitar, *Documenting the Myth of Taino Extinction* [Guitar, Lynne (2002) [33 paragraphs]. *KACIKE: The Journal of Caribbean Amerindian History and Anthropology* [On-line Journal], Special Issue, Lynne Guitar, Ed. Available at: http://www.kacike.org/GuitarEnglish.html [Date of access: 6 January 2008].

22 *HI*, *Obras*, vol. IV, pp. 1345–1355.

23 As noted above, this term is not synonymous with *encomienda* but the names *repartimiento* and *encomienda* are close enough in meaning and application to use interchangeably.
24 *HI, Obras*, vol. IV, p. 1353.
25 *HI, Obras*, vol. IV, p. 1354.

2   Justice for all

1 *HI, Obras*, vol. IV, pp. 1336ff. Other quotes in this section from these pages in the *HI*.
2 Presumably love your neighbors as yourselves, the first being love your God.
3 A *maravedí*, one of the smallest coins in the Hispanic world, like a penny, or better, a halfpenny in the English world of the time.
4 The Great Commission was to spread Christianity to "all nations." Mathew 28:16–20.
5 Daniel Castro in *Another Face of Empire: Bartolomé de las Casas, Indigenous Rights, and Ecclesiastical Imperialism* (Durham, NC: Duke University Press, 2007).
6 Robert Ricard, *The Spiritual Conquest of Mexico: An Essay on the Apostolate and the Evangelizing Methods of the Mendicant Orders in New Spain, 1523–1572* (Berkeley: University of California Press, 1966).
7 These Dominicans were priests as well as friars, having taken the special vows of the Dominican Order in addition to their ordination as priests in the Catholic Church. Not all Dominicans were priests, but brothers in the order without ordination. Only priests were allowed to celebrate and deliver the Sacraments of the Church, such as saying Mass, hearing confessions, performing marriages, etc. There were seven Sacraments observed by the Church.
8 *HI, Obras*, vol. IV, p. 1514.
9 *HI, Obras*, vol. IV, pp. 1519–1520.
10 See Diana Butler Bass, *A People's History of Christianity: The Other Side of the Story* (New York: HarperCollins, 2009), especially "Justice," pp. 184–188, for "justice" as a calling card of the reformist tradition in this time period.
11 *HI, Obras*, vol. V, p. 1760.
12 This sermon is reproduced in many modern versions, but the original from which these passages were drawn is in *HI, Obras*, vol. V, pp. 1761–1763.
13 *HI*, "Esta voz (dixo él) [os dice] que todos estáis en pecado mortal y en él vivís y morís oir por la crueldad y tiranía que usáis con estas inocentes gentes."

14 *HI, Obras*, vol. V, pp. 1761–1763.
15 Lewis Hanke, *All Mankind is One: A Study of the Disputation Between Las Casas and Juan Ginés de Sepúlveda in 1550 on the Intellectual and Religious Capacity of the American Indians* (Dekalb, IL: Northern Illinois University Press, 1974), p. 4.
16 The entire episode from *HI, Obras*, vol. V, p. 1765ff.
17 *HI, Obras*, vol. V, p. 1766.
18 This and the following passages about Hatuey in Cuba from *HI, Obras*, vol. V, pp. 1863–1864. *Lèse-majesté* literally means "injured majesty" and is the crime or offense against a reigning sovereign or against a state.
19 Most of this scene described by Las Casas in *HI, Obras*, vol. V, p. 1879.
20 See Noble David Cook's Chapter 1, "In the Path of the Hurricane: Disease and the Disappearance of the Peoples of the Caribbean, 1492–1518," in Noble David Cook, *Born to Die: Disease and New World Conquest, 1492–1650* (New York: Cambridge University Press, 1998) for how modern research and historiography have basically confirmed what Las Casas witnessed and reported on, although adding an analytical structure based on the modern study of demographics, epidemiology, and the nature and vectors of epidemic diseases not available to Las Casas.
21 Arawaks of Cuba refer to agricultural, politically-organized societies who spoke an Arawakan language at the time of European contact. Arawakan languages were spoken throughout the Greater Antilles and parts of northern South America. Although the Arawakan speakers in Cuba have at times been called "Tainos," that term is more commonly restricted to peoples of Hispaniola and Puerto Rico. Synonyms for the Amerindians of Cuba include "Sub-Taino," "Western Arawaks," and "Ciboney."
22 Email communication from Salvador Larrúa Guedes to L. Clayton, 27 Nov. 2009; see also Felipe Pichardo Moya, *Los indios de Cuba en sus tiempos históricos* (La Habana: A Muniz y Hno., 1945).
23 For a modern view of the effects of disease on the conquest, see David Henige, "Recent Works and Prospects in American Indian Contact Population," *History Compass* 6(1)(2008): 183–206.
24 This and other passages on the process by which Las Casas came to this realization from *HI, Obras*, vol. V, pp. 2082–2084.
25 For a full discussion of the Book of Ecclesiasticus, see the Catholic Encyclopedia online: available at: http://www.newadvent.org/cathen/05263a.htm. Ecclesiasticus is part of the Apocrypha included in Catholic versions of the Bible, but not Protestant ones. Las Casas conflated a number of verses of Chapters 34 and 35 into his remembrance. See especially 34: 23–27, which can be read in English and Latin Vulgate (which Las Casas was most

familiar with) side by side at: http://www.latinvulgate.com/verse.aspx?t=0
&b=26&c=34.

26   *HI, Obras*, vol. V, p. 2082. The full passage reads:

> In confirmation [of his decision] everything he read favored it; he
> [Las Casas, writing characteristically in the third person] used to say
> and affirm that from the moment the blinders were removed from
> his eyes, he never found a book in Latin or Spanish—over the course
> of forty-four years, or thereabouts—that did not provide reason and
> authority which proved and corroborated the justice [of his actions]
> on behalf of the Indians, and which condemned the injustices,
> wrongs, and injuries done to them.

27   Thomas Benjamin, *The Atlantic World: Europeans, Africans, Indians, and
     Their Shared History, 1400–1900* (New York: Cambridge University Press,
     2009) is a good example of how this old subject fits into a new paradigm.
28   *HI, Obras*, vol. V, p. 2101.
29   As usual, drawing from Las Casas's writings himself, in this instance, *HI,
     Obras*, vol. V, pp. 2102ff. But also from the many biographies, including
     Henry Raup Wagner, in collaboration with Helen Rand Parish, *The Life and
     Writings of Bartolomé de las Casas* (Albuquerque: University of New Mexico
     Press, 1967), p. 17ff, A. Huerga, *Fray Bartolomé de las Casas, Obras*, vol. I,
     pp. 76ff; R. Menéndez Pidal, *El padre Las Casas: su doble personalidad*
     (Madrid, 1963), pp. 14ff, M. Giménez Fernández, *Bartolomé de las Casas,
     vol. 1: delegado de Cisneros para la reformación de las Indias* and *Bartolomé
     de las Casas, vol. 2: capellán de S. M. Carlos I, poblador de Cumaná (1517–
     1523)* (Seville, 1960), pp. 52ff, etc.
30   *HI, Obras*, vol. V, pp. 2102ff. This entire scene is described in this section
     of the *HI*.
31   A full copy, in English, of the Laws of Burgos may be found at the following
     web maintained by Professor Peter Bakewell, History, Southern Methodist
     University. Available at: http://faculty.smu.edu/bakewell/BAKEWELL/texts/
     burgoslaws.html.
32   Las Casas recalls this interview in *HI, Obras*, vol. V, p. 2104.
33   *HI, Obras*, vol. V, p. 2107.
34   Giménez Fernández, *El plan*, pp. 104–115.
35   *HI, Obras*, vol. V, p. 2108.
36   Many versions of the Laws of Burgos are available, quite a few online. A
     printed version, albeit old, but by one of the best scholars of the age, is Lesley
     Byrd Simpson, *The Laws of Burgos, 1512–1513: Royal Ordinances for the*

Good Government and Treatment of the Indians (San Francisco: J. Howell Books, 1960; reprinted by Greenwood Books, Westport, CT, 1979).

37   *HI, Obras*, vol. V, pp. 2107–2108; Giménez Fernandez, *El plan*, pp. 115–116.

38   Gutiérrez, *Las Casas*, p. 79, 80. The full text of the *Memorial de Remedios para las Indias* is in *Obras completas*, vol. XIII, pp. 23–48. Gutiérrez used the five-volume edition of the *Obras escogidas* edited by J. Pérez de Tudela, and published in Madrid between 1957–58 in the Biblioteca de Autores Españoles.

39   Wagner, *Las Casas*, pp. 20–22, is devoted to an analysis of the *Remedy*.

40   *Cartas y memoriales*, "Memorial … (1516)," vol. XIII, p. 36, and Gutiérrez, *Las Casas*, p. 324. See Chapter 6 for a full exploration of Las Casas and slavery. Also, a chapter "Addressing the Atlantic Slave Trade: Las Casas and the Legend of the Blacks," by Eyda M. Merediz and Verónica Salles-Reese, in Santa Arias and Eyda M. Merediz, Eds. and contributors, *Approaches to Teaching the Writings of Bartolomé de las Casas* (New York: Modern Language Association, 2008), pp. 177–186; and, most recently, Lawrence A. Clayton, "Bartolomé de las Casas and the African Slave Trade," *History Compass*, Volume 7, Issue 6, Pages 1526–1541. Published Online: 10 Sept. 2009.

3   Social experiments

1   The Hieronymites, founded in 1374 and named in honor of St. Jerome, were one of the principal orders in Spain of the sixteenth century, very austere but devoted to an active ministry.

2   *HI, Obras*, vol. V, 2135.

3   *HI, Obras*, vol. V, pp. 2149–2157 for the account of the first six months of 1517 on Española by Las Casas.

4   *HI, Obras*, vol. V, pp. 2150–2162 for Las Casas's account of his last few months in Española before embarking for Spain, May 17, 1517.

5   My thanks to Professor James Vernon Knight, Anthropology, University of Alabama, for the above. Email communication, August, 2009.

6   Rolena Adorno, *The Polemics of Possession in Spanish American Narrative* (New Haven, CT: Yale University Press, 2008).

7   As you will recognize as you read on, this was well before the celebrated debate on the issue in 1550. See Chapter 6.

8   *HI, Obras*, vol. V, pp. 2177.

9   From Matthew 6: 24. And perhaps this passage from the Apostle Paul's letter
     to his young follower Timothy came to mind:

> People who want to get rich fall into temptation and a trap and into
> many foolish and harmful desires that plunge men into ruin and
> destruction. For the love of money is a root of all kinds of evil. Some
> people, eager for money, have wandered from the faith and pierced
> themselves with many griefs.
>
> (1 Timothy, 10–110)

10   *HI, Obras*, vol. V, 2181.

11   "The chancellor came to have such confidence in the cleric that he wrote
     a long report to the King extolling his experience, ability, and knowledge
     of the affairs of these Indies; and I think he also praised him for his good-
     ness, good wishes, and the rightness of his instincts." *HI, Obras*, vol. V,
     p. 2183.

12   The first time presumably was the mission with the Hieronymites to
     Española that had gone so badly.

13   *HI, Obras*, vol. V, p. 2193.

14   *HI, Obras*, vol. V, pp. 2203–2205.

15   *HI, Obras*, vol. V, p. 2205. It is from Acts 8:20, where Peter responds to a
     sorcerer (Simon) offering money for the gift of the Holy Spirit. "May your
     money perish with you. ..." is the translation in the New International
     Version of the Bible.

16   Wagner, *Las Casas*, pp. 48–49, discusses, convincingly, the effects of the
     discovery of Yucatán by Francisco Hernández de Córdoba, of paved streets,
     stone buildings, and gold, on Las Casas and his contemporaries.

17   For a good summary of Cortés's activities, see A. R. Pagden, editor and
     translator, with an introduction by J. H. Elliott, *Hernan Cortes: Letters from
     Mexico* (New York: Grossman Publishers, 1971). Both Elliott and Pagden's
     long introductory essays set the stage, and supply many of the details, for
     Cortés, his actions in the Indies and how they were paralleled by events in
     Spain.

18   *HI, Obras*, vol. V, pp. 2404–2426 where Las Casas tells of his encounter with
     Quevedo and his appearance before the court. We have used quotes where
     the power of the words need to be preserved exactly as Las Casas recorded
     them (*HI, Obras*, vol. V, pp. 2402–2426) and have paraphrased occasionally
     in the succeeding presentation of this court appearance to preserve the flow
     of the story.

19   *HI, Obras*, vol. V, p. 2411.

20 Gutiérrez, *Las Casas*, pp. 291–299 presents a good summary of the Aristotelian argument, its Spanish and European proponents, and those who, like Las Casas, vigorously repudiated it.

21 "Xevres" was Las Casas's rendition of Charles's Grand Chamberlain, Guillaume de Croy, Lord of Chièvres, a Burgundian who "remained the dominant force in his master's policies until death removed him in 1521," in William Maltby, *The Reign of Charles V* (New York: Palgrave, 2002), p. 12.

22 *HI, Obras*, vol. V, pp. 2413–2414. The editors of the *Obras completas* wondered—as anyone does reading the detail included by Las Casas in this scene—how Las Casas could have remembered it all, especially since some of it was composed decades later. On pp. 2595, of *Obras*, vol. V, footnote #10 they speculate that Las Casas keep a diary or journal, and it was from this source that he was able to recall the detail and immediacy that went into the narrative of the *History*.

23 *HI, Obras*, vol. V, p. 2435.

24 *HI, Obras*, vol. V, p. 2437. Las Casas wrote, "tacitly condemning the 'Mohammetan way' which our people, in entering these lands, had followed."

4   The era of the conquests of Mexico and Peru, 1520s–1540s

1 Giménez Fernández, *Politica inicial*, pp. 942. Las Casas wrote in *HI, Obras*, vol. V, p. 2441, that it was 11 November, but he was off by a few months.

2 See Chapter 6, "The Spanish Invasion," in Michael C. Meyer, William L. Sherman, and Susan M. Deeds, eds., *The Course of Mexican History* (8th ed., New York: Oxford University Press, 2007) for more on the conquest of Mexico, plus a good list of readings.

3 See especially Matthew Restall, *Seven Myths of the Spanish Conquest* (New York: Oxford University Press, 2003) for a useful and readable lineup of the old interpretations of the conquest.

4 George Raudzen, "Main Reasons for Early Colonial Conquest, 1493–1788," in George Raudzen, ed. and contributor *Technology, Disease, and Colonial Conquests, Sixteenth to Eighteenth Centuries: Essays Reappraising the Guns and Germs Theories* (Leiden: Brill, 2001), p. 36.

5 Inga Clendinnen, "'Fierce and Unnatural Cruelty'; Cortés and the Conquest of Mexico," *Representations*, 33, Special Issue: the New World (Winter, 1991): 65–100.

6   He actually may have intended to sail on the same fleet in 1502 that brought Las Casas to the Indies but before it sailed, he fell off a wall outside the window of a lady friend, who happened to be married, and he narrowly escaped death from the cuckolded husband. Injured pretty badly by his amorous escapade, he did not leave until 1504.

7   Many of the "myths" of Spanish invincibility are explored in depth in Matthew Restall, *Seven Myths of the Spanish Conquest* (New York: Oxford University Press, 2003).

8   Hernán Cortés, *Letters from Mexico*. Translated and edited by A. R. Pagden, Introduction by J. H. Elliott (New York: Grossman, 1971), pp. xvii ff.

9   Cortés, *Letters from Mexico*.

10   Cortés, *Letters from Mexico*.

11   The details need not concern us here, although it was an internal dispute for power and authority that marked the differences between Velázquez and Cortés, and the latter had disobeyed Velázquez's orders in 1519 *not* to leave Cuba. Cortés, ambitious and sometimes impetuous, simply ignored the Governor's orders and struck out, essentially on his own, trusting to his arms, his will, and his skills to succeed.

12   Las Casas covers this episode in *HI, Obras*, V, pp. 2443–2447.

13   The irony is, of course, that it was neither Ocampo's or Las Casas's coast, although both claimed the right to work it over, for evil, or for good. Daniel Castro, *Another Face of Empire: Bartolomé de las Casas, Human Rights and Ecclesiastical Imperialism* (Durham, NC: Duke University Press, 2006), does a good job of examining this phenomenon.

14   *HI, Obras*, vol. V, p. 2452.

15   All of the above dialogue in *HI, Obras*, vol. V, pp. 2366–2367.

16   *HI, Obras*, vol. V, pp. 2464–2465. Also, Remesal, *History general*, vol. I, pp. 142–143.

17   *HI, Obras*, vol. V, p. 2608, see explanatory notes # 8 and # 9 by editors of this volume. These two notes are long explanatory notes which follow the tortuous inner deliberations of Las Casas at this moment. I found them—the notes—totally convincing and in line with the narrative—sometimes convoluted—of Las Casas.

18   *HI, Obras*, vol. V, p. 2472.

19   As in so much modern orthography and spelling, the traditional names as spelled have changed to conform more exactly as they may have sounded in the language of the Amerindians, in this case Quechua, the language of the Incas. We have chosen the generally recognized variation in English for comprehension and recognition.

20   Regicide was also a charge, since Atahualpa had his captured brother, Huascar, executed to prevent him from becoming a puppet of the Spaniards.

21   *Obras*, vol. XIII, p. 83.

22   *Obras*, vol. XIII, p. 79.

23   Las Casas's tendency to hyperbole and exaggeration is well exemplified in how he described the land.

24   "Carta a un personaje de la corte," or "Letter to a Person in the Court," Granada, Nicaragua, 15 October, 1535, *Obras*, vol. XIII, p. 92.

5 The New Laws of 1542 and Bishop of Chiapa

1   Henry Raup Wagner, in collaboration with Helen Rand Parish, *The Life and Writings of Las Casas* (Albuquerque: University of New Mexico Press, 1967, p. 41. This and the following quote on the m.o. of Las Casas from Parish. See also R. Menéndez Pidal, *El padre Las Casas: su doble personalidad* (Madrid, 1963), p. 143.

2   Ramón Hernández, O. P., Introduction, "Entre los Remedios … El Octavo," *Obras completas*, vol. X, p. 288.

3   Gustavo Gutiérrez, *Las Casas: In Search of the Poor of Jesus Christ* (Maryknoll, NY: Orbis Books, 1993), p. 400, quoting from the "Anonimo de Yucay, 1571," pp. 106–107. The document "Anonimo de Yucay, 1571" probably authored by a Dominican, García de Toledo, is very critical of Las Casas. See pp. 396ff of Gutiérrez, *Las Casas*, especially the footnotes, for an extended discussion of this document and how it fits into the anti-Lascasian rhetoric of the times.

4   Gutiérrez, *Las Casas*, p. 400.

5   Gutiérrez, *Las Casas*, p. 402, citing the "Anónimo … ," p. 401.

6   A. Huerga, *Fray Bartolomé de las Casas, Obras*, vol. I, p. 206.

7   Huerga, *Las Casas, Obras*, vol. I, p. 206.

8   Huerga, *Las Casas, Obras*, vol. I, p. 208.

9   Biermann, "Bartolomé de las Casas," in Juan Friede and B. Keen, editors, *Bartolomé de las Casas in History: Toward an Understanding of the Man and His Work* (DeKalb, IL: Northern Illinois University Press, 1971), p. 468.

10   Biermann, "Bartolomé de las Casas," pp. 468–469.

11   That story is told in its entirety in a much longer biography of Las Casas due to appear in 2011, published by Cambridge University Press.

12   Giménez Fernández "A Biographical Sketch," p. 100 in Juan Friede and B. Keen, editors, *Bartolomé de las Casas in History: Toward an Understanding*

of the Man and His Work (DeKalb, IL: Northern Illinois University Press, 1971).

13   Note # 34, p. 234, Huerga, *Las Casas*, quoting from G. Fernández de Oviedo, *Historia general de Indias*, lib. 33, cap. 54, ed. J. Pérez Tudela, BAE 120, pp. 263–264. BAE is Biblioteca de Autores Españoles, Madrid, Rivadeneira y Atlas, 1864.

14   Remesal, *History* general, p. 334.

15   Carta al Principe don Felipe (15-9-1544), Santo Domingo, *Obras*, vol. XIII, p. 185.

16   Carta al Principe don Felipe.

17   This whole account encompassed between pp. 99–104 of *Diario de Fray Tomás de la Torre, 1544–1545, Desde Salamanca, España, hasta Ciudad Real, Chiapas, 424 dias hacia S. Xbal de Fr. Bartolomé de las Casas*. Notes by Franz Blom (Chiapas, Mexico: Gobierno Constitucional del Estado de Chiapas, 1974). This diary was used by Antonio de Remesal, O.P., for his monumental *Historia de la provincial de San Vicente de Chiapas and Guatemala*, first published in Madrid, 1619.

18   *Diario*, pp. 111–112.

19   Wagner, pp. 132ff.

20   Huerga, *Las* Casas, p. 246.

21   Wagner, *The Life and Writings*, p. 134.

22   Regidores and alcaldes were town officials, sometimes translated as town councilors. The chief alcalde is sometimes translated as the mayor.

23   Wagner, pp. 136ff describes it well, and I have followed Wagner, who based his narrative, as was his custom, on a strong documentary basis, and I have compared it as well to the account in Huerga, p. 247ff.

6   "All mankind is one:" on the nature of humans, servitude, and slavery

1   Lewis Hanke, *All Mankind is One: A Study of the Disputation Between Bartolomé de las Casas and Juan Ginés de Sepúlveda in 1550 on the Intellectual and Religious Capacity of the American Indians* (DeKalb, IL: Northern Illinois University Press, 1974), p. 58. Also, Henry Raup Wagner, in collaboration with Helen Rand Parish, *The Life and Writings of Las Casas* (Albuquerque: University of New Mexico Press, 1967), pp. 170ff.

2   Hanke, *All Mankind is One*, p. 59.

3   Hanke, *All Mankind is One*, p. 67.

4   Stuart B. Schwartz, *All Can Be Saved: Religious Tolerance and Salvation in the Iberian Atlantic World* (New Haven, CT: Yale University Press 2009), brings to light that not all Spaniards conformed to orthodox Christian principles, so there was plenty of room for debate on how exactly one was saved within the Christian theology.

5   Hanke, *All Mankind is One*, p. 62.

6   Menéndez Pidal, pp. 207–208. Even Menéndez Pidal contends that Sepúlveda exaggerated the incapacities of the Indians and the "superior culture" of the Spanish.

7   R. Menéndez Pidal, *El padre Las Casas: su doble personalidad* (Madrid, 1963), p. 208.

8   Hanke, *All Mankind is One*, p. 66.

9   Hanke, *All Mankind is One*, p. 67.

10 Hanke, *All Mankind is One*, p. 68

11 Hanke, *All Mankind is One*, p. 85.

12 Hanke, *All Mankind is One*, pp. 85–86.

13 Hanke, *All Mankind is One*, pp. 85–86.

14 A. Huerga, *Fray Bartolomé de las Casas, Obras*, vol. I, p. 271, citing, in footnote # 29, De Sepúlveda, J. G. "Proposiciones temerarias, escandalosas y heréticas que notó el Doctor—en el libro de la conquista de Indias que fray Bartolomé de las Casas, obispo que fue de Chiapa, hizo imprimir sin licencia en Sevilla, año de 1552," en Fabíe [see Huerta bibliography for full citation to Fabíe], vol. II, 543–569.]

15 Hanke, *All Mankind is One*, p. 93.

16 Hanke, *All Mankind is One*, pp. 97ff. This and the following six interrogatives beginning with "where" all from the same page in which Hanke quotes the *Defense* of Las Casas.

17 Hanke, *All Mankind is One*.

18 Hanke, *All Mankind is One*, p. 76.

19 See Santa Arias and Eyda M. Merediz, *Approaches to the Teaching the Writings of Bartolomé de las Casas* (New York: Modern Language Association, 2008), which contains, for example, at least one chapter devoted to the subject of Las Casas and slavery; Eyda M. Merediz and Verónica Salles-Reese, "Addressing the Atlantic Slave Trade: Las Casas and the Legend of the Blacks;" also L. A. Clayton, *Bartolomé de las Casas and the African Slave Trade, History Compass*, Volume 7, Issue 6, Pages 1526–1541. Published Online: 10 Sep 2009.

20 John Thornton, *Africa and Africans in the Making of the Atlantic World* (2nd edn.) (Cambridge: Cambridge University Press, 1998). See especially his Chapters 1–3 for the European dimension to the establishment of the slave trade.

21   See Thornton, *Africa and Africans in the Making of the Atlantic World*; David Eltis, *The Rise of African Slavery in the Americas* (New York: Cambridge University Press, 2000); Bernard Bailyn, *Atlantic History: Concept and Contours* (Cambridge, MA: Harvard University Press, 2005); Herbert Klein, *The Atlantic Slave Trade* (Cambridge: Cambridge University Press, 1998).

22   Thornton, *Africa and Africans in the Making of the Atlantic World*, pp. 74, 94–96.

23   Klein, *The Atlantic Slave Trade*, p. 13.

24   Egerton, Games, *et al.*, *The Atlantic World*, p. 59, a useful insert labeled "Early Iberian Slavery."

25   Slightly paraphrased from where Las Casas wrote in his *Historia de las Indias, Obras completas*, vol. V, pp. 2190–2191, when explaining his role in promoting the importation of Negro slaves from Castile to the Indies: "since some of the Spaniards on this island told the cleric Las Casas—realizing what he wanted and that the Dominican friars did not want to absolve those who had Indians if they weren't freed—that, if he could get a license from the King to bring a dozen Negro slaves from Castile, this would allow them to free the Indians, and remembering this the cleric. ..." Las Casas completes the thought by saying he then included this desire expressed by the settlers in his memorial to the King proposing to bring some blacks slaves from Castile to Española to help free the Indians.

26   *HI, Obras*, vol. V, pp. 2190–2191. See also Isacio Pérez Fernández, *Bartolomé de las Casas ¿contra los negros?* (Madrid: Edit. Mundo Negro, México: Edic. Esquila, 1991).

27   Rolena Adorno, *The Politics of Possession in Spanish American Narrative* (New Haven, Ct: Yale University Press, 2008), pp. 64ff.

28   Las Casas, *Obras completas*, vol. V, p. 2191.

29   Las Casas, *Obras completas*, vol. V, p. 2324.

30   Parish and F. Sullivan, *De Unico Vocationes: The Only Way by Bartolomé de las Casas* (New York: Paulist Press, 1992), pp. 203–204, quoting from *Historia de las Indias*, lib. 3, caps. 102, 129).

31   Parish and Sullivan, *Bartolomé de las Casas*, Addendum III, "Las Casas' Condemnation of the African Slave Trade;" Thornton, *Africa and Africans*, pp. 24–25 for more on Gomes Eannes de Zurara.

32   Parish and Sullivan, *Bartolomé de las Casas*, pp. 204–208. Eanes sometimes spelled Eannes.

33   Parish and Sullivan, *Bartolomé de las Casas*, pp. 204–208.

34   Parish and Sullivan, *Bartolomé de las Casas*, pp. 204–208.

35 See G. Gutiérrez, *Las Casas: In Search of the Poor of Jesus Christ*, translated by Robert R. Bar (Maryknoll, NY: Orbis Books, 1993), pp. 321ff.

36 My thanks to Steve Newton, then an MA candidate in History at the University of Alabama, for undertaking some research on the theory and practice of just war as interpreted by St. Augustine.

37 Gutiérrez, *Las Casas*, p. 322, footnote # 68, citing his own "La Iglesia y los negros," and J. F. Maxwell, *Slavery and the Catholic Church*, and J. Dutilleul, "Esclavage."

38 Gutiérrez, *Las Casas*, pp. 326–330.

39 *Obras*, vol. V, p. 2324. Translation by Parish and Sullivan, p. 203; also in Gutiérrez, *Las Casas*, p. 327.

40 Author's translation. In the *Obras*, vol. V, p. 2191. As for the *dio primero* phrase, or "first gave that advice," see Gutiérrez, *Las Casas*, pp. 573–574, footnote 96, who explains the context quite convincingly in the following passage:

> The expression *dio primero* has been curiously interpreted—against all historical and literal evidence—as meaning that Bartolomé had been *the first to make* the petition he now reproves. Surely it is obvious, especially in view of the context, that the declaration is part of his retraction; what he held *in the past* ("primero") is not his view today.

See also Parish and Sullivan, *Bartolomé de las Casas*, p. 202 and Gutiérrez, *Las Casas*, p. 327.

41 Parish and Sullivan, *Bartolomé de las Casas*, p. 208; original *Obras*, vol. III, p. 475, which is Book I of the original *History*.

42 Parish and Sullivan, *Bartolomé de las Casas*, p. 208;

43 Gutiérrez, *Las Casas*, p. 329.

44 See, for example, Klein, *The Atlantic Slave Trade*, p. 184; Egerton, *et al.*, pp. 462–463.

45 For the traditional beginning of the abolitionist movement, see, for example, David Brion Davis, *Slavery and Human Progress* (New York: Oxford University Press, 1984), pp. 129ff which dates the beginnings of the end of the slave trade to the second half of the eighteenth century.

46 Wagner, pp. 187–188.

47 Huerga, *Las Casas*, p. 288. Huerga's footnote 36 cites Gonzáles Montes, "La interpretación protestante de la conquista y evangelización de América. Una visión que perdura," *La ciudad de Dios*, 205 (1992), pp. 359–389.

48   Huerga, *Las Casas*, p. 19.
49   Las Casas, *Obras*, vol. 10, p. 19, Introduction by Ramón Hernández, O.P., to the works published in 1552, in which Hernánez quotes from *Obras*, vol. 2, *De unico vocationis modo*, pp. 378–380.
50   Parish, "Las Casas," p. 48.

Bibliographic Essay

The documentary sources

The latest and most complete compilation of Las Casas's works is *Fray Bartolomé de las Casas: Obras completas* [*Complete Works*] (14 vols., Madrid: Alianza Editorial, 1992). Some of these volumes number well over 1000 pages each. While not all are Las Casas's works (the entire first volume, for example, is a biographical study by Alvaro Huerga), the output is impressive. Almost all the quotes in this book attributable to Las Casas are drawn from the *Obras completas*.

Many of Las Casas's tracts and polemics were composed in Latin, and these are published in the original Latin in the *Complete Works*. Fortunately, the editors of the series translated all the Latin into Spanish and the texts appear side by side so the modern reader can make his own comparisons.

Of his immense output, a few of his most important works have been translated into English. His *Brief History of the Destruction of the Indies* was first published in Seville in 1552, but soon found itself in print in translation throughout Europe in the sixteenth and seventeenth centuries, all part of the great struggle between Catholics and Protestants for the soul of Christianity. The latest one in English, with one of the best introductions to the subject is *An Account, Much Abbreviated, of the Destruction of the Indies, with Related Texts*, edited and with an introduction by Franklin W. Knight and translated by Andrew Hurley (Indianapolis: Hackett Publishing, 2003).

For the most complete study of this work, see *Fray Bartolomé de las Casas: Brevísima relación de la destruición de las Indias* (Bayamón, Puerto Rico:

Universidad Central de Bayamón, Centro de Estudios de los Dominicos del Caribe, Instituto de Estudios Históricos Juan Alejo de Arizmendi, 2000), with an almost 400-page critical preliminary study by Isacio Pérez Fernández. Included in this exhaustive 1055-page volume are a previously unpublished version of the *Relación* from 1542, plus two other versions which represented modifications and additions made in 1546 and 1552. A copy of the *Brevísima* is in volume X of the *Obras completas*.

In English, the best example of Las Casas's diverse works is an anthology of his writings put together by George Sanderlin, first published in 1971 and subsequently reissued in 1992. *Bartolomé de las Casas: A Selection of His Writings* (New York: Knopf, 1971) and *Witness: Writings of Bartolomé de las Casas* (Maryknoll, NY: Orbis Books, 1992) are basically the same book, although the latter contains a new Foreword by Gustavo Gutiérrez on "The Theological Perspective of Bartolomé de las Casas." English-only readers will find either of these anthologies a good guide to Las Casas's thoughts and actions in his own words, always the most compelling source of any biography.

Chunks of Las Casas's writings that have attracted particular scholars' attention have made it into print in English. For example, Helen Rand Parish produced a beautifully illustrated edition of Las Casas's long letter to the Emperor Charles V, written sometime in the fall of 1543, on matters pertaining to Las Casas's appointment as Bishop of Chiapa. This booklet, *Las Casas as a Bishop: A New Interpretation Based on his Holograph Petition in the Hans P. Kraus Collection of Hispanic American Manuscripts* (Washington, DC: Library of Congress, 1980), is an exhaustive examination of Las Casas's life at the time he became Bishop of Chiapa, drawing upon materials in the Library of Congress.

Parish (editor) and Francis Patrick Sullivan (translator) collaborated to bring Las Casas's first book to the English-speaking world. *De Unico Vocationes: The Only Way by Bartolomé de las Casas* (New York: Paulist Press, 1992). This book, with an excellent Introduction by Parish, frames the intellectual and spiritual rationale for Las Casas's defense of peaceful evangelization as the "only way" legitimately to claim any sort of sovereignty and control by Spaniards over Amerindians.

After the *Brief Destruction of the Indies*, Las Casas's most famous contribution to history is probably his rendition of the diary of Columbus's first voyage to the New World, which Las Casas included in his *History of the Indies*. The original diary was lost and so the only record of this path-breaking first voyage is in the *History*. The best modern rendition is Oliver Dunn and James E. Kelley, Jr., *The Diario of Christopher Columbus's First Voyage to America, 1492–1493, Abstracted by Bartolomé de las Casas* (Norman and London: University of Oklahoma Press, 1989).

For those interested in digging deeper into the debate at mid-century between Las Casas and Sepúlveda, Stafford Poole, C.M., basing his work on earlier efforts, finished the job of translating Las Casas's famous *In Defense of the Indians* (DeKalb, IL: Northern Illinois University Press, 1974). A Foreword by Martin E. Marty (to the paperback edition, published in 1992) and Poole's own editorial introduction set the stage for this fascinating window into how Las Casas's mind worked. Over three hundred pages long, it is one of the best original sources of Las Casas's writing. To help the modern student even more, Lewis Hanke wrote *All Mankind is One: A Study of the Disputation between Bartolomé de las Casas and Juan Ginés de Sepúlveda in 1550 on the Intellectual and Religious Capacity of the American Indians* (DeKalb, IL: Northern Illinois University Press, 1974; paperback, 1994) as a companion volume to Poole's *In Defense of the Indians*.

And, of course, if one can read Spanish, then a plunge into the Spanish archives—some of them online (see "The Electronic Las Casas" below)—is always a thrill, seeing and touching and reading the originals. But there is enough of Las Casas published largely in the *Complete Works*, and supplemented by English language translations of many of his major works, to get on with many research topics set in the early colonial period.

The biographies

Biographies of Las Casas have appeared with regularity since the early seventeenth century, when Antonio de Remesal, a Dominican friar, produced the first one, *Historia general de las Indias Occidentales y particular de la gobernación de Chipas y Guatemala* (Guatemala, 1932; first published Madrid, 1619). This is a general history of the Dominican Order in southern Mexico and Guatemala, but with a biography of Las Casas running like a thread through it. In the mid-twentieth century, studies of Las Casas became almost an academic growth industry as students of human rights, the Indians of America, revisionists of the Conquest, and others approached 1966, the 400th anniversary of his death.

His fellow Spaniards have produced the most hagiographic, as well as the most critical, biographies. His most devoted student was Manuel Giménez Fernández, a fellow Sevillan, whose two huge volumes (each close to 1000 pages) on Las Casas's life between 1517 and 1523 are exhaustive studies of a short span in the life of the man and his times. These are *Bartolomé de las Casas, vol. 1: delegado de Cisneros para la reformación de las Indias* and *Bartolomé de las Casas, vol. 2: capellán de S. M. Carlos I, poblador de Cumaná (1517–1523)* (Seville, 1960). Giménez Fernández died before completing the full biography, but his

174   *Bibliographic Essay*

vast erudition and total devotion to Las Casas reflected the immensity of his subject.

Among the most critical biographies was the one produced by the distinguished philosopher-historian Ramón Menéndez Pidal, whose *El padre Las Casas: su doble personalidad* (Madrid, 1963) attacked Las Casas as being a single-minded fanatical anti-Hispanicist, in his lifelong devotion to the American Indians.

Standing like a giant among Lascasian studies in the twentieth century is, however, not a Spaniard, but an American, Lewis Hanke. Hanke "discovered" Las Casas while working in the archives of Spain in the early 1930s. In 1948, Hanke published a seminal study entitled *The Spanish Struggle for Justice in the Conquest of America* (latest version, Dallas, TX: Southern Methodist University Press, 2002). It still is a basic book for any student wishing to learn more about the subject. Hanke, however, never wrote a formal biography of Las Casas.

The other American of near equal stature to Hanke associated with Lascasian studies is Benjamín Keen. Keen's own works, including Juan Friede and Keen, editors, *Bartolomé de las Casas in History: Toward an Understanding of the Man and His Work* (DeKalb, IL: Northern Illinois University Press, 1971), and Keen, *Essays in the Intellectual History of Colonial Latin America* (Boulder, CO: Westview Press, 1998), which paralleled in scope and erudition Hanke's lifetime output, although no one matched Hanke in sheer volume of works on Las Casas's themes and issues.

Another American, Henry Raup Wagner, in collaboration with Helen Rand Parish, wrote a carefully documented biography, *The Life and Writings of Bartolomé de las Casas* (Albuquerque: University of New Mexico Press, 1967) that is still a standard in English, although out of print. Helen Parish, long an admiring student of Las Casas, wrote her own biography, *The Untold Story*, but, as of 2011, it remains unpublished. Parish died in 2005. Her papers were donated to the Bancroft Library at the University of California, Berkeley in 2008.

The Peruvian Dominican, Gustavo Gutiérrez, one of the pioneers of Liberation Theology in the mid-twentieth century, wrote *Las Casas: In Search of the Poor of Jesus Christ*, translated by Robert R. Barr (Maryknoll, NY: Orbis Books, 1993). In a *tour de force*, Gutiérrez portrayed Las Casas as a forerunner of Liberation Theology. This is an immensely sympathetic biography. It is especially good and detailed on Las Casas and the great battle in the 1550s between the *encomenderos* desiring perpetuity and Las Casas and his supporters.

Finally, in the genre of general biographies, Alvaro Huerga wrote *Fray Bartolomé de las Casas*, a complete biography that appeared as the first volume of the *Obras completas*. Although rather selective in content, it portrays Las Casas not only with sympathy, but also with his many flaws.

The issues

Not only was Las Casas a prolific writer, but his life has generated a vast outpouring of often controversial literature on the man and his times that often reflects vastly different points of view on the Encounter/Conquest era. The historical literature, of which only a small percentage can be included in this short essay, easily bears out his diverse interests and career.

In the mid-twentieth century, as Americans struggled with overcoming centuries of racial prejudice and discrimination in which the modern Civil Rights movement was born, scholars such as Lewis Hanke sought to probe the origins of racism in the Western world and they found in Las Casas's life much to consider.

Hanke, in *Aristotle and the American Indians: A Study in Race Prejudice in the Modern World* (Bloomington and London: Indiana University Press, 1959), tangled with Aristotle, as did Las Casas in his debate in 1550 with Sepúlveda, questioning Aristotle's division of men into those born to govern, and those born to be governed, one of the cornerstones of slavery and modern racism. This book is really much more about Las Casas than Aristotle, and frames one of Las Casas's greatest contributions over his lifetime to the concept that all men share equal rights in both Scripture and natural law.

The Black Legend was explained and analyzed in a lively exchange of essays almost half a century ago by Lewis Hanke and Benjamin Keen. Hanke, "More Heat and Some Light on the Spanish Struggle for Justice in the Conquest of America," *Hispanic American Historical Review* 44(3) (1964): 293–340; and Keen, "The Black Legend Revisited: Assumptions and Realities," *Hispanic American Historical Review* 49(4) (1969): 703–719; Hanke, "A Modest Proposal for a Moratorium on Grand Generalizations: Some Thoughts on the Black Legend," *Hispanic American Historical Review* 51(1) (1971): 112–127; and Keen, "The White Legend Revisited: A Reply to Professor Hanke's 'Modest Proposal,'" *Hispanic American Historical Review* 51(2) (1971): 336–355, should all be read by students interested in this phenomenon.

The 1992 Quincentennial commemorating the 500th anniversary of the discovery of America by Christopher Columbus spawned a growth industry of publications "exposing" and "revising" the history of the age of exploration and conquest. Las Casas was both pilloried and praised in the outpouring of history and polemics. A good example of the polemical literature was Kirkpatrick Sale's *The Conquest of Paradise: Christopher Columbus and the Columbian Legacy* (New York: Knopf, 1990), which borrowed in part from Las Casas's Black Legend to magnify and distort the negative consequences of the European invasion of America. Sale and Las Casas viewed the Conquest/Encounter through the same lens even though separated by almost five hundred years.

Modern historians, anthropologists, and demographers, on the other hand, in research aimed at discovering the true basis of the Encounter, unencumbered by polemics and national, religious, and racial prejudices, for example, criticized Las Casas for wild exaggeration of atrocities and the population estimates he made. David Noble Cook, *Born to Die: Disease and New World Conquest, 1492–1650* (Cambridge: Cambridge University Press, 1998), is one of the most balanced and thorough of these new studies, while William M. Denevan, ed., *The Native Population of the Americas in 1492* (2nd ed., Madison: University of Wisconsin Press, 1992) is but another example of many books and articles in this genre.

While scholars took their shots at Las Casas, the most violent attack came from a fellow Spaniard, Ramón Menéndez Pidal, whose biography of Las Casas mentioned above, *El padre Las Casas*, not only condemned Las Casas for his extreme and often violent criticism of his fellow countrymen, but also for defending the Amerindians with an equal abandonment of balance and good judgment. The points of view represented in this work are a perfect example of the White Legend that came into existence in the early twentieth century, defending the actions of the Spanish in the Conquest as heroic, valiant, well-meaning, and even devoutly Christian.

Lascasistas were astounded at these criticisms and often responded in kind with hagiographic studies that portrayed Las Casas in almost equally exaggerated terms, only this time in his favor. Helen Rand Parish's studies, such as the two listed above, *The Only Way* and *Las Casas as a Bishop*, and others like *Las Casas en México: historia y obras desconocidas* (México: Fondo de Cultura Económica, 1992), fall into this category, although her writing was always based on deep research in the archives, often uncovering new documents written by Las Casas or his contemporaries.

Less polemical, but no less pro-Lascasista, was the intellectual and spiritual study of Las Casas's life by a fellow priest and Dominican, the Peruvian Gustavo Gutiérrez, published in 1993, his *Las Casas: In Search of the Poor of Jesus Christ* (1993, see above). Gutiérrez, in fact, is one of the founders of the Liberation Theology movement, having defined it and even given it its name in his pathbreaking *Teología de liberación: perspectivas* (Salamanca: Ediciones Sigueme, 1972) and as translated by Robert McAfee Brown, *Gustavo Gutiérrez: An Introduction to Liberation Theology* (Maryknoll, NY: Orbis Books, 1990).

The Quincentenary era also saw the appearance of Las Casas's *Obras completas* mentioned above. It was largely conceived of, compiled, edited, and written by his Dominican brothers in Spain and, as such, they viewed him favorably. These heavily annotated volumes are the first place for anyone to start in their research on Las Casas. The first volume, a full-scale, original biography by

Alvaro Huerga (see above in Biographies) was, nonetheless, not hagiographic but balanced in its approach and interpretation of Las Casas's life.

One of the most intriguing questions in Las Casas historiography is why did he do what he did? Why did he turn into such a passionate defender of American Indians, liberty, and human rights when hundreds, then thousands, of his fellow countrymen witnessed and lived the same scenes he did in the Indies? This question is answered in various commentaries in the *Complete Works* and I tend to agree with his fellow Dominican brothers. At the core of his inspiration and drive was a spiritual awakening, born in the reformist Christian milieu in which Spain was living in the fifteenth and sixteenth centuries. Daniel Castro, however, takes another view in his interesting and provocative *Another Face of Empire: Bartolomé de las Casas, Human Rights and Ecclesiastical Imperialism* (Durham, NC: Duke University Press, 2006). In Castro's view, Las Casas was in fact an imperialist, but one with a religious twist.

Literary scholars have frequently focused on Las Casas as well. Eyda M. Merediz and Santa Arias coordinated and contributed to a volume, *Approaches to Teaching the Writings of Bartolomé de las Casas* published by the Modern Language Association (New York, 2008), that contains many different views and interpretations of Las Casas. It is a compilation of modern, largely literary, approaches to Las Casas, demonstrating that he does not belong to historians alone, but that his life and times have universal appeal.

In literature, Rolena Adorno's *The Politics of Possession in Latin American Narrative* (New Haven: CT: Yale University Press, 2007) deals in large part with Las Casas as polemicist and traces his influence across the centuries by assigning the rationale of Spanish claims to sovereignty and dominion in the New World amid the narrative tradition.

In a lighter vein, there was even a cartoon Las Casas in the 1990s. This was the "Las Casas Light" side to the Quincentennial, although certainly not in reference to Las Casas's character, but rather to the comic book style strips that appeared about the time of the Quincentennial.

The electronic Las Casas

Las Casas lives on, on the Internet. The principal portal into Lascasiana on the web is www.lascasas.org. The site has numerous sections, including links to various pages and sites devoted to Las Casas, such as a link to the Biblioteca Virtual Miguel de Cervantes/ Biblioteca Americana/Bartolomé de las Casas, one of the most complete sources for online resources devoted to Las Casas.

In this virtual library (www.cervantesvirtual.com/bib_autor/bartolomedelas casas/) one can navigate easily to many of his original works now digitized, as well as to major secondary works of books and articles (some even in English), and to images—especially graphic ones of the Black Legend by the illustrator Theodore de Bry—and other resources.

The www.lascasas.org site contains the newest books, articles, and conference papers given on Las Casas as well as some longer articles that are biographic in nature, and an entire page devoted to links to other Las Casas's pages and institutes named in his honor.

PARES (or Portal de Archivos Españoles) is the online portal to the archives in Spain, and one can easily navigate to the various archives with major Las Casas holdings. The online address is: http://pares.mcu.es A simple search using "Bartolomé de las Casas" produced hundreds of references to documents in at least nine Spanish archives, many with the digitized documents (letters, petitions, etc.) online.

Final note

In the search for the history and significance of Las Casas, the resources and bibliographic base are vast. Suffice to mention one last tome devoted to works about Las Casas. In 1981, the Centro de Estudios de los Dominicos del Caribe (CEDOC) of Bayamon, Puerto Rico, published Isacio Pérez Fernández's 928-page *Inventario documentado de los escritos de Fray Bartolomé de las Casas*, or "annotated inventory of the writings of Las Casas." It is a work of love and erudition that provides an entry by year and document (manuscript or published) to a high percentage of everything that Las Casas produced over his lifetime.

Index

Note: Page numbers in *italics* refer to figures and maps. A forward slash indicates continuous treatment of a topic that is interrupted by a full page figure or map.

Printed in the United States
By Bookmasters